Alexander Mantouche

Influence of mythologemes on the genre group of adventure cinema

Alexander Mantouche

Influence of mythologemes on the genre group of adventure cinema

ScienciaScripts

Cover image: www.ingimage.com

This book is a translation from the original published under ISBN 978-620-2-08166-5.

Publisher:
Sciencia Scripts
is a trademark of
Dodo Books Indian Ocean Ltd. and OmniScriptum S.R.L publishing group

120 High Road, East Finchley, London, N2 9ED, United Kingdom
Str. Armeneasca 28/1, office 1, Chisinau MD-2012, Republic of Moldova, Europe
Printed at: see last page
ISBN: 978-620-8-01800-9

CONTENTS.

INTRODUCTION

The "adventure" genre is the most popular among moviegoers worldwide. [1]The ten highest-grossing films in the history of the global box office are represented exclusively by this genre: "Avatar, Titanic, Avengers, Fast and Furious 7, Harry Potter and the Deathly Hallows, Cold Heart, Iron Man 3, Avengers 2, Transformers 3: Dark Side of the Moon, Lord of the Rings: The Return of the King [64]. [64]. The 20 most profitable films at the global box office are also entirely represented by adventure films. The highest-grossing films from eleventh to twentieth place: "007: Skyfall Coordinates", "Transformers: Age of Extinction", "The Dark Knight:
Legend Reborn, Pirates of the Caribbean: Dead Man's Chest, Toy Story: The Great Escape, Pirates of the Caribbean: On Stranger Tides, Jurassic Park, Star Wars. Episode I: The Hidden Menace", "Alice in Wonderland", "The Hobbit: An Unexpected Journey". [64]. The list of the fifty highest-grossing films at the global box office is also represented exclusively by the adventure film group [46; 47; 64]. Talking about this group of genres, we can't help but notice its great influence on mass culture, although it is not its most brilliant component.

Adventure films encourage their target audiences to take an interest in culture, history, art, mythology, religion and literature. As a rule, after the release of a popular adventure film, the book market experiences a boom in sales related to the film's theme, and the media begin to actively cover the issues raised in the film's plot. In other words, adventure films are an effective stimulus to the cognitive activity of their viewers, and set the fashion for a certain historical or cultural phenomenon.

The great popularity of the adventure film genre with viewers all over the world, and the significant impact it has on its very impressive audience, make adventure cinema a universal phenomenon, understandable by different cultures.

In his treatise "Poetics", Aristotle notes that "the best of all is the recognition arising from the events themselves, and the astonishment of the public is due to the natural course of events..." [2, P. 33]. [2, C. 33]. This idea of the ancient Greek

[1] Since May 2015.

philosopher, even twenty-three centuries later, is fully confirmed by adventure films: the correspondence between plots and the events themselves

The fact that an adventure genre belongs to the historical and cultural experience of humanity determines the understanding and acceptance of the plots of these images practically outside the temporal and territorial frameworks of national cultures.

The problem of the correspondence between adventure stories and the life and cultural experience of society has been actively debated in various scientific disciplines (anthropology, cultural studies, ethnography, comparative mythology, psychology, philosophy and art history). These studies have traditionally relied on myths and archetypes as the "foundation" of storytelling. In recent decades, the study of mythologemes has attracted growing interest from researchers in the humanities, who see myths similar in plot and values as the generation of a basic fabula based on a logically ordered sequence of archetypes. The very term "mythologem" was introduced into scientific exchanges by C.Kerenyi and C.G.Jung, who understood it as "mythological foundation" [43, P.20] - "mythological foundation" [43, P.20] - "mythological foundation" [43, P.20] - "mythological foundation" [43, P.20] - "mythological foundation" [43, P.20]. [43, P. 20] - the primary fabula that constitutes the meaning of a myth or mythological image: "... it is not simply a question of 'causes', but rather of primary substances or primary states that never grow old, can never be overcome and produce everything and always" [43, P. 18] [43, C. 18].

The study of mythologemes has long been associated exclusively with the name of C. Kerenyi, who studied the mythologemes of ancient Greek gods and heroes.

At the turn of the twentieth and twenty-first centuries, the active study of mythologemes by scientists in various countries began to be observed, and the question of mythologemes in human cultural and social life aroused growing interest. However, despite the growing interest in this subject, the question of the influence of mythologemes on contemporary art has been little studied.

Thus, the scientific novelty of this article lies in the fact that mythologemes, as basic fabulae widely represented in the adventure film genre group, have not been actively considered in scientific work on film studies.

The relevance of this Master's thesis lies in the fact that the subject of the influence of archetypes and mythology on adventure cinema, which is close to the designated theme of mythologemes, is the subject of active research in domestic and foreign film studies, and that the theme of mythologemes itself is gaining in popularity among scientist-ethnographers, philologists, philosophers and culturologists.

The practical importance of this work most likely lies in the use of the results of this master's thesis in the curricula of students in profile specialties at creative educational institutions, as well as in the methodology of script development in commercial cinema.

The **subject of** this Master's thesis is Belarusian cinema of the adventure genre. The **subject of the** research is mythologemes, myths and archetypes as plot-forming factors in adventure films.

The **aim of** this thesis is to create a systematic understanding of the basic fabulae of Belarusian adventure cinema and their correlation with similar examples of foreign adventure cinema.

To achieve this goal, the following **objectives** have been identified:

1. Identify the main mythologems, archetypes and myths that influence the adventure film genre.
2. Study the structural regularities of mythologemes that influence the construction of adventure film plots.
3. Study the influence of mythologemes, myths and archetypes on adventure cinema.
4. Characterize how mythologems are used in films.
5. Reveal the specific characteristics of mythologemes, myths and archetypes used in Belarusian adventure cinema.

The following points are put forward for the defense:

1. Mythologemes, myths and archetypes have a notable influence on the adventure film group.

2. Belarusian adventure cinema is in line with global trends, using the same archetypal sequences as foreign films of a similar genre.

3. Cyclic tetrachotomy is performed in four parts

The psychological organization of the hero image is the main mechanism for analyzing the presence of mythologemes in cinema.

CHAPTER 1
HISTORIOGRAPHY AND RESEARCH METHODOLOGY

The problems of myth and archetypes in cinema have been the subject of extensive scholarly work, considering almost every possible mode of interaction between primordial mythological images and cinematic art. However, there are virtually no studies devoted to the problem of mythologemes in cinema.

If we consider the historiography of the study of basic fabulae (as a kind of synonym for the concept of mythologemes) influencing plot composition, one of the first to attempt to identify and systematize the universal bases of plot was the French director and man of the theater J. Polti, who published "Thirty-six Dramatic Situations" in 1856. After studying 1,200 works and 8,000 actors [20, P. 113- 117], Polti hypothesizes that every work, whether legend, myth, novel, short story or play, rests on 36 basic fabulae, which he proposes: "Plea, Rescue, Revenge (following a crime), Revenge (of a loved one for a loved one), Afflicted, Sudden misfortune, Sacrifice of someone, Riot, Daring attempt, Kidnapping, Riddle, Realization, Hatred between loved ones, Rivalry between loved ones, Adultery (accompanied by murder), Madness, Fatal indiscretion, Unintentional incest, Unintentional murder of a loved one, Sacrifice of self in the name of an ideal, Sacrifice of self for the love of one's own, Sacrifice of immense joy, Sacrifice of one's own in the name of duty, Rivalry of unequals, Adjuster, Crime of love, Dishonor of the beloved, Love (encountering obstacles), Love for an enemy, Ambition, Struggle against God, Unfounded jealousy, Judicial error, Remorse of conscience, Newly found, Loss of one's own" [20, P. 115-116].

In the national arena, Polti's opinions were sanctified in his articles by a Soviet statesman, the People's Commissar for Education of the RSFSR, writer and art historian A.V.Lunacharsky, who evaluated the book as follows: "For all its paradox, the book ("36 dramatic situations") deserves attention and can be useful." [The interest of J. Polti's book lies in the fact that for each "dramatic situation", the author proposes a basic fabula in addition to a set of actors.

The early twentieth century was characterized by numerous cultural, ethnographic and psychological studies that raised questions about intercultural interaction and the influence of historical experience on creativity. This era was characterized by active attempts to introduce ideas from psychoanalysis, analytical psychology, oriental and exotic cultures into global mass culture. One of the most significant works of this period is J.J. Fraser's "Folklore in the Old Testament", which establishes in the biblical myths of the Old Testament plot patterns identical to the folklore of different peoples in Europe, Africa, Asia, Oceania and America. By comparing numerous examples of plots from different mythologies corresponding to the biblical myths of the Old Testament, the author has created a logical model of the primary fabulae of the genesis of man, the fall into sin, the "seal of Cain", the great flood, the Tower of Babel, the treaty between God and Abraham, etc. [37]. As Fraser has summarized each myth with a basic fabula, it seems appropriate to consider this work in the context of the historiography of the study of mythologemes.

The study of universal plots was developed by the Swiss psychiatrist and founder of analytical psychology C.G.Jung, who proposed the theory of archetypes - images of the collective unconscious, which, according to Jung, was the source of universal symbolism. The influence of archetypes on folklore and theater was developed in his scientific work by K.G.Jung's associate, the Swiss philologist and religious scholar K.Kerenyi. Studying the influence and use of archetypes in myth and art, Kerényi and Jung published a monograph in 1941 entitled "Introduction to the Essence of Mythology" (later included in the book "Soul and Myth. Six Archetypes"), and introduced the category of "mythologeme", which forms the basis of this dissertation. The term they introduced refers to the basic universal mythological fabulae that are ubiquitous in the cultures of the world's different peoples [43].

Jung and Kerényi considered myth to be the basis of human culture, drawing active parallels between mythology and musical art (and its basic models). The importance of this work in the historiography of the subject studied is primarily due to the fact that "Introduction to the Essence of Mythology" was the first work to raise the question of the influence of mythologemes on the composition of the fabric of folk and literary works.

The ideas expressed by Kerenyi and Jung in "Introduction to the Essence of Mythology" and "Soul and Myth" were further developed by the American anthropologist J.J. Campbell. In his work on comparative mythology, Campbell came to the conclusion that the absolute majority of folk sources, as well as neo-mythological stories, have a common compositional basis, which he called a monomyth. According to Campbell, a monomyth is a cyclical structure that includes the following stages of story development: "the everyday world, the hero's call, the hero's rejection of the call, induced action/supernatural help, the hero crossing the first threshold, the whale's belly, the path of trials, the meeting with the goddess, reconciliation with his father, the apotheosis, the reward at the end of the journey, the refusal to return to the everyday world, the magical escape, the rescue from the outside, the crossing of the threshold of the everyday world, the lord of both worlds, the freedom to live" [18, p. 42-43]. [18, C. 42-43]. Curiously, Joseph Campbell's work inspired George Lucas to create his famous "Star Wars" cinematic hexalogy.

Mythologems were studied in Soviet science by V.P. Goran, who in 1990 published the work "Ancient Greek Mythologeme of Fate", in which the author studies the mythologem of fate as a fact of the genesis of the mythological and literary tradition of the ancient world. According to Horan, the mythologem is. a generative idea that exists by continuity in the cultural life of a society. [8]

The question of archetypes in adventure genres has been addressed by G.F. Iaccino, who has published scholarly work on the influence of archetypes on the horror film genre ("Psychological Reflections on Cinematic Terror: Jungian Archetypes in Horror Films", 1994) and on the science fiction and fantasy genre ("Jungian Reflections within the Cinema: A Psychological Analysis of Sci-Fi and Fantasy Archetypes", 1998). The main concept of Iaccino's research is the correlation of character models and stories with Jungian archetypes [54, 55].

The Astrology of Film: The Interface of Movies, Myth, and Archetype" (2004), in which the author attempts to reveal the influence of myths on the composition of cinematic stories [61], is close to the theme of mythologemes in cinema.

In "Action Figures: Men, Action Films, and Contemporary Adventure Narratives" ("Action Figures: Men, Action Films, and Contemporary Adventure Narratives", 2006), American film scholar M. Gallagher explored the evolution of the genre film hero, addressing the basic plot of adventure films. His research is based on archetypes and types of male heroes, their emergence, development and perspectives, as well as their interaction and correlation with female heroes (heroines), the isolation of "masculine" and "feminine" genders and the study of trends towards the interpenetration of these genders [50].

Another American film scholar, Geoffrey Hill, in Illuminating Shadows: The Mythic Power of Film (Geoffrey Hill, 1992), compares cinema to Jung's ideas on dreams, which reflect the collective unconscious, while also touching on the theme of recurring motifs in story construction and characterization [52].

L.I. Gornitskaya ("The mythologem of the island in Russian literature: genesis, structure, semantics" [9]), V.G.Turkina ("Mythologem of the hero and mass consciousness" [34]), M.N.Izvorska-Elizarieva ("Myth. Music. Mozart. 'Magic Flute' - cosmogonic mythologem" [15]), A. A.Batueva ("Mythologem of good and evil in Indo-European languages" [4]), L.A.Guluk ("Mythologem of femininity in Silver Age culture" [10]). A number of publications by Belarusian and Russian academics have been devoted to questions of mythologemes in the context of national cultures: "The Mythologeme of Unclean Power in the Silver Age" [4].
culture traditionnelle des Biélorusses" by E.A.Rutsky [28] (article in the collection "Outantychny falklore: prablemy vyvuchennya, zahavannya, peraimannya"), "Mythologeme of woman-fate in ancient Celts and Germans" [23] (collection of articles edited by T.A.Mikhailova). [23] (collection of articles edited by T.A. Mikhailova).

At the turn of the twentieth and twenty-first centuries, foreign works devoted to the study of mythologems were published: "Mythologems: Incarnations of the Invisible World" by J. Hollis [53], "Myth - Mythologeme - Medea: The

Transformation of the Figure of Medea in the Novel of Christa Wolf in Comparison with the Interpretation of the Myth by Euripides" by K. Luther, "Journey Beyond the Fringe - Adaptations of Ancient Roman Mythologems in Medieval Folklore" by B. Burkhardt. However, it is important to note that these works consider mythologems in the context of ethnography, philosophy and philology, without taking into account their interaction with cinematic art.

It is important to note the post-Soviet works devoted to archetypes in cinema: "Archetypes in Cinematography" by K.S. Karchevskaya [17], "Archetypal Foundations of the Culture of the Turn of the XX-XXI Cc. N.S.Vdovushkina [6], "Archetypal Foundations of the Hero Image in the Dramaturgy of Russian Cinema: (on film material from 1986-2012)" by M.A.Sharapova [6]. M.A. Sharapova [42].

Other sources used in this Master's thesis include Russian film studies, in particular Semyon Israelievich Freilich's Theory of Cinema: From Eisenstein to Tarkovsky, in which the author devotes considerable attention to the definition of genre and style within the framework of art history [36].

In his book "Cinema Between Hell and Heaven", A. Mitta examines genre conventions and protagonist archetypes [22]. In particular, Mitta proposes four main archetypes of the protagonist in modern cinema: "our acquaintances", "the outsider", "lost souls" and "idols". The fact that these archetypes fit into the general quaternary model of the basic mythologem discussed in chapter two may be considered curious.

In "Psychology for Screenwriters: Constructing Conflict in Plot", W. Indyk considers the practical use of ideas from Z. Freud (Oedipus complex, neurotic conflict, stages of psychosexual development, ego defense mechanisms and dream semantics), E. Erikson (normative conflict and identity crisis), C.G. Jung (character archetypes and plot archetypes), J. Campbell (monomyth) and J.A. Erikson (normative conflict and identity crisis). Erikson (normative conflict and identity crisis), C.G.Jung (character archetypes and story archetypes), J.Campbell (monomyth), A.Adler (inferiority complex, sibling rivalry, lifestyles) and R.May (existential conflict) [16].

In "Million Dollar Story", R. McKee structures and systematizes the compositional patterns of film drama, behavioral reaction patterns, value orientations and structural interrelationships between characters [21].

It's worth noting a number of publications in periodicals devoted to archetypes in cinematic art, both in the post-Soviet space and in the practice and theory of Western cinema. The most interesting articles are "The Diamond Hand", "Kurochka Pryaba" and The Russian Dream. A psychiatrist's free reflections on a favorite film" by A. Danilin [11], "Intellectual auteur cinema as a European idea" by N. Samutina [31], "When heroes pass into eternity" by O. Artemyeva [3] and "Lifting the mask: types, archetypes and the casual human being" by D. Corbett [49].

The number of such publications, especially in the context of electronic resources, is considerable, but it's fair to say that these publications reveal the question of the correlation between archetypes and cinema without addressing the questions of mythologemes or archetype sequences, which could be considered certain mythologemes.

The theoretical and methodological basis of the research is thus formed by the works of art history and cultural studies of Russian and foreign scholars who have studied the subject of this thesis - mythologemes, as well as archetypes, genres and patterns of story composition in the context of genre groups.

In line with the objectives of this thesis, the following methods were required: phenomenological,
deductive, iconographic.

This chapter has therefore reviewed the bibliography relating to the question of mythologemes and the influence of mythologemes on cinema in both domestic and foreign works. Although there are a large number of works devoted to archetypes in cinema, as well as to mythologemes as basic fabulae, which are logical continuations of archetypes in the context of folklore and philology, relatively few works are devoted to the theme of mythologemes in the context of cinema. However, as mentioned above, a sufficient number of studies have been devoted to the question of archetypes and mythology in cinema.

A review of the literature revealed a fragmentary and incomplete study of the subject of this master's thesis. Certainly, there are more than enough studies devoted to the related subject of the archetype and its correlation with cinematic art, but very few studies have been devoted to the mythologem in the context of cinema.

The subject of this work - Belarusian adventure cinema - was considered by the researchers primarily in the context of the historiography of Belarusian feature films, which is the subject of a large number of publications.

The subject of this thesis work - mythologem, myth and archetype as plot-forming factors in the adventure film genre - has been considered by a number of researchers as a cross-cultural factor in the context of psychology, cultural studies and mythology. The connection between the object and subject of this Master's thesis and the work of other researchers has not been revealed.

In addition to literary sources, this work used documents from periodicals devoted to cinema, publications from Internet resources on subjects relevant or close to this Master's thesis, as well as film documents.

CHAPTER 2

MYTHOLOGY IN ADVENTURE FILM

2.1 Characteristics of the adventure film genre

As we saw above, the adventure film group is the most popular with audiences at the global box office. The active acceptance of adventure films is clearly due to the public's need for psychological relief, caused by the lack of "dangerous experience" derived from adventure and thrills. It's unlikely that an ordinary person, in unusual circumstances, would single-handedly confront a gang of criminals, foreign special services, mystical events and so on. The phenomenon of the adventure hero's popularity is based on the public's psychological paradox. Most people lead ordinary, measured lives, which leads them to want to "get out" of everyday reality, to dream of adventure and extreme experiences. However, adventure and extreme experiences in people's real lives are unjustified risks that can rightly be avoided. Adventure films are therefore the safest and most accessible way of compensating for desired taboo experiences.

It therefore seems logical that the popularity and commercial success of the adventure film group is due to the psychology of the audience's perception of them (including the fact that the stories told in adventure films correspond to expectations of the course of events). It's also important to remember that the earliest feature films in cinema history were the vérité films of Georges Méliès, the forerunners of adventure films, which allows us to suggest that adventure genres in cinema are the genres with the longest history of interaction with their viewers.

The adventure film group includes a large number of film genres, such as adventure, western, cloak-and-dagger, detective, noir, thriller, action, disaster, horror, fantasy, science fiction and heroic-patriotic war. We should also mention adventure films for children, which are most often a variant of the adventure, fantasy, science fiction or heroic-patriotic genre.

Adventure films traditionally tell of exciting adventures, misadventures or adventures of characters who can't live a quiet, measured life because they've been involved in some kind of adventure. In fact, the definition of "adventure film" is rather complex, but the canon of this genre is expeditions, exotic locations, exciting stories about unusual experiences.

Westerns and their ideological analogues (cloak-and-dagger films, or "swashbucklers", as they are known in foreign film studies) are characterized by the development of the story in a world where the laws of life are harsh, sometimes brutal. The Wild West, where westerns are traditionally set, is the land of anarchy, where the extremes of human nature are most actively manifested. However, a Western doesn't have to be set on the West Coast of the United States in the 19th century. A western can be a picture that recounts events in a certain region with dashing manners in another era. The same is true of "cloak-and-dagger" films, whose distinctive feature is that the action takes place in 17th- and 18th-century Europe, and instead of shooting revolvers and Winchesters, the heroes fight with swords.

The action film is the most "monochrome" of the adventure film genres. The hero of an action film is a solitary hero who confronts unequal forces.
of an exaggerated evil. Two-dimensionality" and satisfaction orientation
The need for violence suggests that the roots of the militant film lie in bloody medieval amusements and vulgar popular theaters, in which all the The action has been reduced to a confrontation between "very good" and "very bad" heroes by beating the antagonist by the protagonist.

The thriller is a genre of suspense film based on the transmission of intense excitement to the viewer (the name of the genre is derived from the English word thrill). Thrillers rarely constitute an independent film genre. There are crime thrillers, mystical thrillers (combined with the horror genre), noir thrillers, hybrids between thriller and action, sometimes romantic thrillers (i.e. hybrids between thriller and melodrama) and comic thrillers.

The horror film genre is ideologically similar to the thriller, but differs in its desire to evoke a sense of fear in the viewer. The motifs traditionally used to evoke fear include supernatural forces, xenomorphic life forms and maniacs.

Noir", also ideologically close to the thriller genre, is the most "psychological" of the group of adventure genres. "The hero of the noir novel is a lost soul, alien to both "correct" society and the values that oppose it.

Historical, fantasy and science-fiction adventure films are generally a reflection on the socio-political structure of the modern world, a search into the historical past or the creation of an analogy with the political and social realities of the present in an imaginary or fictional world of the future. An interesting feature of the science-fiction film tradition that cannot be overlooked is the predominance of the social utopia in Soviet cinema and the dystopia in foreign cinema. The traditions of science fiction subgenres - fantasy and superhero stories - are often linked to a rigid canon in which the hero confronts the ruler of an anti-utopian world, with a clear dichotomy between good and evil. This situation sets the paradigm for the story's development, with reference to myths and sagas featuring heroes.

The detective is a genre that traditionally deals with criminal investigations, as well as espionage "games" played by agents of certain special services. Detectives are often strictly regulated by the genre canon, which dictates the obligatory composition of characters (as in the classic English detective) or the plot of the work (as in the spy detective).

Disaster films are a sub-genre of adventure cinema, recounting the misadventures of the hero or of humanity as a whole, caused by a natural, man-made, technogenic, microbiological or anthropogenic disaster. A frequent motif in disaster films is the hero's rescue of loved ones or comrades on board ship or aircraft in distress, in disaster zones, from radiation or viral contamination.

Since it's unlikely to create a coherent story across the genres and sub-genres of the adventure group, based solely on traditional adventures (chases, fights, shoot-outs and other "active action"), the adventure film resorts to an active synthesis of genres. Most often, this synthesis is based on the genres of the adventure group itself, and combines, for example, action and crime, horror and disaster. However, it's also important to note the interaction with other genres outside one's own genre group.

Interaction with the comedy and melodrama genres is the most common. Motifs from other genre groups are extremely important, as they help to create a more authentic story and motivation for the characters, and images of characters and events that are close to and understandable by the audience. The interpenetration of the adventure and comedy genres is fundamental to this group. The enrichment of the adventure genre with comic and melodramatic elements contributes to the broadening of film audiences and the understanding of film plots by different age and gender groups [50, p. 162-164].

In addition, many actors play archetypal characters in comedy and adventure films to great effect. On this occasion, S. Freilich remarked: Gérard Philippe, in the naive adventure film "Fanfan-Tulipe", most strikingly embodied the Gallic character, and A. Kuznetsov - the character of the Russian soldier in a parody of Vladimir Motyl's western "The White Sun of the Desert"""". [36, C. 129]. We can conclude that the perception of adventure roles as "swan songs" in the acting career of this or that artist is due to the specificity of the perception of the adventure genre. The viewer unconsciously strives to identify with the hero of adventure cinema, and so, in his or her memory, such a role will be identified with the image of the most interesting and holistic acting work, rather than with the image of the hero of "higher" genres.

In his book "Acting Figures: Men, Action Films and Contemporary Adventure Narratives", Gallagher draws attention to the following points: the adventure and action film has always been a "masculine" genre, tolerating and exploiting stories of male heroism created by male filmmakers for a fundamentally male audience. The most intriguing evolution of the genre in the 1990s has been the incorporation of formal elements associated with the 'feminine' genre of melodrama" [50, C. 45]. According to Gallagher, the active synthesis of the comedy genre and the action film is due to the popularity of Hong Kong comedy action films (whose main star was Jackie Chan), which conquered the action segment of the film market at the turn of the 1980s-1990s [50, p. 160].

It's important to note that adventure films, westerns and cloak-and-dagger movies have been using genre synthesis practically since their inception. Action, thrillers and horror films have only recently begun to interact with other genres. In general, the adventure film group tends to replace the "pure" varieties of this group with their "synthetic" analogues, which make active use of comic and melodramatic motifs. Thus, the main characteristic of adventure cinema is its active interaction with the genres of comedy and melodrama.

If we consider adventure cinema in terms of its stimulating function, we can affirm that it has a direct impact on the cognitive activity of spectators, on the creative activity of authors, as well as on increased sales in the book, leisure and tourist services markets. Examples include the increase in excursion activity in New Zealand during the filming of "Lord of the Rings", and the heightened interest in Oxford among tourists during the filming of "Harry Potter".

To sum up the importance of the adventure genre group for mass culture in general and cinema in particular, it's worth noting the following facts:

1. Adventure films are the most sought-after and commercially successful of all film genres.

2. The adventure film genre allows audiences to experience the dangerous thrills and spills of ordinary life.

3. The group of adventure films is often the most effective for developing actors' careers and creating vivid images accepted by audiences as the most successful acting work.

4. The adventure genre group is characterized by active interaction with the comedy and melodrama genres.

5. The adventure genre group stimulates the cognitive activity of its audience, getting them interested in the issues raised in the film's plot (art, culture, history, religion, science, etc.).

6. The adventure film genre effectively stimulates purchasing activity, influencing first and foremost tourism (including the commercial spheres linked to tourist activity), the markets for books, souvenirs and video media intended for home viewing.

Of course, we can't claim that only adventure genres allow viewers to experience taboo subjects, or that only adventure cinema stimulates the audience's cognitive and purchasing activities. However, it is the adventure genre that has the greatest effectiveness on these issues, as well as greater character understanding and audience reaction.

2.2 Mythologem, myth and archetype as story-forming factors

The plots of films about similar events often have the same fabulae, which leads us to hypothesize that they are all based on a certain mythologeme - a common primary fabula. The difference between several literary, dramatic or cinematographic works often lies in a different set of plots and hero "masks" meticulously elaborated by man. The essential differences lie in the external environment (everyday life, appliances, transport, technology, political and economic realities) and in the perceptive superstructures of social morality (attitudes to the family, marriage, sex, xenophobia, gerontophobia, etc.).

If we consider the question of the influence of mythologemes on cinematic plots, it's necessary to raise the issue of archetypes and myths. Obviously, an archetype is a type of hero, a type of situation or a type of hero's reaction to a situation. A mythologem is a basic fabula that is a sequence of archetypes. A myth is an extended narrative that expands and completes the basic fabula with specific images and cultural particularities of a certain society. If we clarify the essence of each of these concepts, we can note the following: archetype - primary image-type, myth - narrative, mythologeme - basic fabula.

The relationship between myth, archetype and mythologem seems to be as follows. An archetype is a certain image that characterizes the hero, his behavior or his situation. A mythologem is a narrative algorithm, i.e. a logical sequence of archetypes that create a basic series of events. A myth is a complete narrative that develops and completes the mythologem algorithm that gave rise to it, with images of heroes, their daily lives and their social and cultural environment.

Traditionally, archetypes are key symbols - images that reflect the specific order and worldview of the film hero. The most common archetypes are Mother Earth (Mother of God), the Heavenly Father (God, Sun or Sky), the protector (traditional hero), the jester ("trickster"), the "Fool of Fools" (apotheosis of human stupidity and ignorance), the little man, the pariah (the "superfluous man"), the rebel (the "man of the shadows"), the little man, the pariah (the "superfluous man"), the rebel (the "romantic hero"), the good rascal (the deceiver forced to survive by deception), the cunning rascal, the virtuous martyr, the hypocritical conqueror (the Antichrist).

In his article "Cinema as Rehabilitation of Archetypal Reality" published in the journal "Film Studies Notes", N. Khrenov concludes "three theses related to the activity of archetypal consciousness in its various manifestations, which cannot be ignored when analyzing the structure of narrative and the spectator's reception of cinema. 1. The identification of the activity of archetypal consciousness requires a specific consideration of cinema, namely: it must be seen in the context of the opposition taking place in the history of art. 2. The activity of archetypal consciousness in cinema is a consequence of the revival in twentieth-century history of the type of culture called by P. Sorokin the culture of the ideal type. 3. The activity of archetypal consciousness in cinema is the flip side of the lowering of the beginning of the author, what R. Barth has called "the death of the author" [39]. [39] . Based on this idea, the archetype is a means of creating a film hero comprehensible to a large mass of viewers, forcing the author to align the hero, his actions, his social and cultural environment with the corresponding typical images of national, regional or world culture.

Hero archetypes in cinema most often appear as embodiments of typical social roles. As mentioned above, A. Mitta, in his book "Cinema Between Hell and Heaven", cites four protagonist archetypes: "Our Acquaintances", "Underdog", "Lost Souls" and "Idols". "Our Acquaintances" is.

A type of hero similar to the most ordinary people. "Underdog" - a hero who wants to change his social status. "Lost souls" - "lost sheep" in the Christian tradition, i.e. these heroes are analogues of "our acquaintances", the only difference being that "lost souls" have chosen the wrong path to reach their goal. The "idols" are "eaters" of desperate situations. [22, C.74-82]

In examining Hollywood cinema, W. Indyk cites R. May's views on the archetypes of the "age of narcissism" reflected in key images of the North American film industry.May's views on the archetypes of the "age of narcissism" reflected in key images of the North American film industry: "American hero" (independent individualist), "cowboy" (lone hero following a code of honor), "lone knight" (hero fighting evil and corruption alone), "rebel cop" (lawman breaking the rules in the name of duty), "gangster" (anti-hero of the megalopolis), "Private detective" (symbiosis of "gangster" and "rebel policeman"), "Contradictory policeman" (policeman who refuses bribes, but does not denounce his corrupt colleagues), "Mad scientist" (solitary genius playing God), "Created monsters" (creatures created and exploited by an irresponsible creator) [16, pp. 293-305].293-305]. It's also worth noting that the most comprehensive catalog of Hollywood archetypes can be found on the tvtropes.org website. However, we cannot avoid the fact that some examples of archetypes in North American cinema turn into clichés and stereotypes (which is most often observed in the horror, science fiction and action film genres), which is rather damaging for the films in which this tendency can be observed.

As far as archetypes as types of situation or types of hero's reaction to the situation are concerned, the motifs of bargaining with the devil, bargaining with conscience, sacrifice for salvation, deceiving the devil, etc. appear more often than others. The archetype of a situation is a certain event perceived by the audience (bearer of the culture) as having one possible way of resolving an action, unambiguous in its motives and evaluation. The sequence of action archetypes constitutes the fabula on which myths (both ancient myths, which have come down to us from the depths of the centuries, and modern myths) are built.

Myths in cinema are also widespread. Although most myths in adventure cinema belong to neo-mythology (new-age mythology), mythological motifs from the ancient world and the traditional folklore of various ethnic communities are present in cinema. Given the influence of myths, we can observe a curious transformation of ancient mythological images in modern cinema. For example, many dystopias echo the ancient Greek myth of the rapture of fire. The protagonist of the dystopia seeks to free people from the oppression and deception of the ruling elites, in which he is extremely similar to Prometheus, whose aim was to save people from the arbitrariness of the Olympian gods. The essential difference is that the end of Prometheus' modern analogues is not as sad as that of their mythological prototype. It's also worth noting that similar myths (the theft of fire and the transmission of knowledge to the human race), with similar values and roughly the same series of events, can be found in many of the world's national cultures.

This trend is particularly interesting for myths that are close in terms of series of events and value attitudes, as these mythological stories allow us to consider them in the context of mythologemes - their original generative fabulae. The most frequent mythologemes in the adventure genre group are the mythologemes of the great mystery, the defender of the nation, the prodigal son, the hypocritical conqueror and the brothers in love with the same woman.

The mythology of the great secret. The hero accidentally receives the "key" to the "great secret" in his hands, but does not understand the true meaning of this "key". Against his will, the hero engages in a conflict with the antagonist who defends the "great secret". The hero discovers the true meaning of the "key" and even manages to investigate the mystery. The hero and antagonist openly dispute possession of the "great secret". The hero solves the riddle and, having defeated the antagonist, becomes the holder of the "great secret".

The most striking examples of films in which the mythology of the great mystery can be clearly traced are Mackenna's Gold (1969, J. Lee Thompson), Treasure Island (1988, directed by David Cherkassky), Treasure Island (2011, directed by Steve Barron), Da Vinci Code (2006, directed by Ron Howard),
"The Adventures of Tintin: The Secret of the Unicorn (2011, directed by Steven Spielberg), Harry Potter and the Sorcerer's Stone (2001, directed by Chris Columbus), Harry Potter and the Chamber of Secrets (2002, directed by Sheldon Lettice), The Ninth Gate (1999, directed by Roman Polanski), Sahara (2005, directed by Breck Eisner), National Treasure (2004, directed by Breck Eisner), The Order (2001, directed by Sheldon Lettice), The Ninth Gate (1999, directed by Roman Polanski), Sahara (2005, directed by Breck Eisner), National Treasure (2004, directed by John Turteltaub),

It's important to note that the mythology of the great mystery is relatively young. This mythologem begins to take shape in European culture at the time of the Crusades (with the emergence and spread of the chivalric orders), develops at the time of the great geographical discoveries (with the discovery of the New World) and consolidates at the turn of the 19th and 20th centuries (on the wave of the growing popularity of the adventure literary genre).

Mythology of the defender of the nation (corresponds to the biblical myth of Moses and the historical figure of Arminius). The hero, raised as an enemy of his people, witnesses the oppression of his tribesmen. He tries to negotiate diplomatically to obtain clemency from the members of his tribe, but is met with hostility from his comrades and decides to fight for them, betraying his "brothers in arms". The hero prepares an uprising and cleverly lures the antagonist into a dangerous situation, where he destroys him and frees "his people".

The most striking examples of films in which the mythologizing of the defender of the nation can be clearly traced are "Equilibrium" ("Equilibrium", 2002, directed by Kurt Wimmer), "V for Vendetta" ("V for Vendetta", 2006, directed by James McTeague), Avatar (2009, directed by James Cameron), The Prince of Egypt (1998, directed by Brenda Chapman, Steve Hickner and Simon Wells), James McTeague), Avatar (2009, directed by James Cameron), The Prince of Egypt (1998, directed by Brenda Chapman, Steve Hickner and Simon Wells). The modified mythology of the nation's protector can be found in Cipollino (1961, directed by Boris Dezhkin), Braveheart (1995, directed by Mel Gibson), Les Druides (Vercingétorix, 2000, directed by Jacques Dorfmann), Animal Farm (1999, directed by John Stephenson).

The myth of the prodigal son. The hero feels dissatisfied with his situation and decides to change his usual way of life in the name of material prosperity. The hero succeeds materially but becomes spiritually poor. He loses his material status and realizes that his true worth was betrayed at the start of his journey to wealth. The hero "returns home".

The most striking examples of films in which the mythology of the prodigal son can be clearly traced are Kramer contre Kramer (1979, directed by Robert Benton),

Big (1988, directed by Penny Marshall), What About Bob? (1991, directed by Frank Oz), Les compères (1983, directed by Francis Weber), Les compères 2 (Un jour mon père viendra, 2011, directed by Martin Valente).

Mythology of the hypocritical conqueror. A vain and cruel hero, vexed at not having obtained power over a certain sphere or territory, decides to destroy the one who has. The hero pretends to win his adversary's favor and places maximum trust in him. The hero overthrows the opponent and obtains the desired power. The hero is overthrown by the defenders of the hero's defamed enemy, and the enemy returns to the throne.

This mythologism is most often found in the images of antagonists. Typical examples of this mythologem are realized in the plots of Horrible Woo ("Arthur and the Minimates"), Lord Voldemort ("Harry Potter"), Vice-Chancellor Dupont ("Equilibrium") and others. Transformed variants of this mythologem include the plots of the wolf in Little Red Riding Hood, Signor Tomato in Cippolino and other insidious fairytale villains.

Mythology of brothers in love with the same woman (the oldest example is the love triangle: Osiris - Isis - Set). Two brothers fall in love with the same girl. Each brother tries to attract the attention of the chosen one, but she chooses the noblest. The rejected brother, humiliated, hunts down his lucky rival, kills him and tries to take his place. The chosen one rejects the bad brother and goes to seek her husband in the afterlife, bringing him back to life.

The clearest examples of films based entirely on the mythology of brothers in love with the same woman are Fatal Passion (The Immigrant, 2013, directed by James Gray), Despicable (Scorned, 2013, directed by Mark Jones), This Means War (2012, directed by McGee).

The last two mythologems are most often realized in subplots linked to the antagonists. The mythologems of the prodigal son, the protector of the nation and secret knowledge are most often used as the basis for the main plot linked to the protagonist. It's worth noting that mythologemes generally exist as basic plots linked to the protagonist, so the influence of mythologemes on artworks is revealed through the protagonist or through the dichotomous protagonist-antagonist pairing. The following examples confirm this idea. The mythologem of the creation of the world, and the mythologem of the creation of man, revolve around the figure of the creator (the god or gods who inhabited the protoworld - the primary cosmos). The mythology of the sinful fall is based on the transmission of the story of created man and his antagonist (the messenger of the gift/source of immortality and its opposite - the gift/source of mortality and perishable existence). The mythology of the gift of fire is inconceivable without the figure of a hero (god or demigod) sympathetic to the heavy burden of the human race.

The mythologem of fate revolves around the figure of the hero, condemned to do exactly what fate has ordained. In other words, the essence of mythologemes is to focus on the hero, whose fate and actions reveal the basic generative plot.

In examining the mechanisms by which mythologems influence cinematography, we have noticed the same organization of the protagonist's image in the mythologems we have encountered, which we have proposed to designate by the term "cyclic tetrachotomy". By "cyclicity", we mean a plot imperative in which, following the denouement, the hero, transformed by the events of the story, must return to the initial state, but in a new, progressive quality. By "tetrachotomy" we mean the four basic states or qualities through which the hero must pass to come full circle, i.e. the cyclical nature of the story. The very definition of "tetrachotomy" is formed from "tetra" - "four" and "tomos" - "division" and, by analogy with the definition of "dichotomy" (bifurcation, successive division into two parts opposed to each other), implies the division of the whole into four parts, each of which opposes the other three.

In his book "The Million Dollar Story", R. McKee proposes, in the chapter "The Principle of Antagonism", a method for working on the plot of the screenplay, based on the negative progression of the change of values in the story: from positive to limit, then to opposite and marginal - extremely negative, carrying a double negative charge (McKee refers to this value as the "negation of negation") [21, P. 321-334]. According to McKee, "history, which in its development reaches the limit of human experience through a deep and wide conflict, must pass through all the stages of the model" [21, P. 322] [21, C. 322].

The four-cycle cyclical progression is also present in J. Campbell's The Hero with a Thousand Faces. Although Campbell himself considers every story to be a variation of a single imperative monomyth based on 27

In the hero's three-act journey, his psychological characterization develops in four clearly distinct stages: flaw, humility, despair and self-sacrifice. In the article "Blockbuster: Archetypes and Acts", D. Proskurov also draws attention to this four-act pattern of change in the archetypes of the "hero with a thousand faces". Proskurov designates the stages of Campbell's hero development by "Jungian" categories of archetypes: 'Orphan', 'Vagabond', 'Warrior' and 'Martyr'" [25]. [25].

Orphans" are both orphaned characters (i.e. children deprived of parents or guardians by the will of circumstance) and childless fathers/mothers, disgraced politicians, workers/employees who have lost their jobs, artists who have lost their recognition, outcasts, and so on. The hero becomes an "orphan" by losing a certain value at the beginning of the story, which is most often the main positive value of the story itself or directly linked to it. The "wanderer" is a type of hero who tries to adapt and get used to circumstances, preferring flight to struggle, trying not to notice the obvious inconsistency between reality and initial expectations. From the point of view of the story's value progression, such a hero evolves towards a passive limit state of value orientations. The transformation of the hero into a "warrior" involves a "baptism of fire", when the hero is forced to renounce his initial values and replace them with opposing ones. Finally, the "Martyr" archetype implies a hero who is prepared to take the riskiest and most reckless action, since it is only by committing an act of self-sacrifice that the hero will be able to achieve the story's main objective.

The hero's motivation in cyclic tetrachotomy can be based on Adler's "life styles": the receiving type, the avoiding type, the controlling type and the socially useful type. At the beginning of the story, the hero generally represents the receiving type: he is deprived of something, but accepts the role imposed on him from outside, without doing anything to improve reality. The second stage of the hero's development is characterized by a transformation into an avoidant type: the hero finds himself in an even more difficult or abusive situation, 28

However, he's not prepared to try to remedy the situation. The accumulated pressure of circumstances on the hero leads him to want to dominate his oppressors (circumstances or other characters), which is a characteristic of the controlling type. Finally, when the hero realizes that he is the antithesis of his initial ideals, he experiences an altruistic desire, signifying a transition to the socially useful type.

The hero's self-awareness in cyclic tetrachotomy appears as a complex of existential crises, according to R. May. The hero is first in the "Innocence" stage, not realizing the crisis phenomena in his world, he is passive, not noticing or ignoring problems, not seeking to change anything for the sake of changing the situation. Then, when the hero re-evaluates his values under the pressure of circumstances, he moves on to the "Rebellion" stage: he's still passive, but already has an external goal. The third stage of the hero's development corresponds to the stage of "ordinary self-awareness", when the hero highlights the problem, the means of solving it and dedicates himself to a meaningful external goal. The final stage - "creative self-consciousness" - is characterized by the hero's revelation of himself; first of all, the hero removes self-delusion from awareness of himself and his goal [16, p. 284-288].

The cyclical tetrachotomy in relation to the hero's identity can be developed on the basis of E. Erikson's views on normative conflict and identity crisis. Erikson's "Trust vs. Distrust" stage is characterized by the hero's naivety and credulity, passivity, distrust and sometimes cynicism. The second stage - "Autonomy versus shame and doubt" - transforms the hero from a distrustful, credulous individual into a rebel, ready to defend the right to autonomy. The third stage - "Initiative versus guilt" - is characterized by a new cycle of development for the hero, caused by guilt over his excessive passivity or, on the contrary, his activity. The fourth stage 29

In the "Zeal against feelings of inferiority" stage, the hero commits an act of self-sacrifice, exposing his personal well-being to knowingly excessive risk in the name of a lofty goal [16, p. 119-129].

It's important to mention Carl Gustav Jung's scientific views in the field of psychology, which also correlate with the examples considered of the hero's development in the context of plot development, and according to which the whole (the integral personality) is made up of four parts - two pairs of opposites that ensure balance [11, p. 186]. [According to Jung, these opposites are the Persona, the Master (Goddess/Old Sage), the Shadow and the Object of Love (Anima/Animus). From the point of view of plot influence, this model plays the role of the hero's control logic - a kind of subconscious "gray cardinal" of the hero. So, in the initial stage, the hero is a "Persona" - the hero as he is, with his usual lifestyle and worldview. The development of the plot takes the hero to the level of "teacher" - the hero learns to survive, adapting to new and unusual conditions. As the plot develops, the hero is confronted with the desire to destroy the forces of antagonism, becoming identical to the "Shadow" - the ideological opposite of the "Persona". Finally, at the end of the story, the hero realizes that because of his actions as "Shadow", his object of love - "Anima" - must suffer, and he takes action to save it, returning to the positive values of creation.

Summarizing the examples discussed above, it can be said that there is an apparent uniformity in the main driving forces of the protagonist in the above models, which influence the compositional structure, setting and thrust of the story. Comparing the models of Jung, May, McKee, Campbell, Adler and Erkson, it can be argued that they all describe the same pattern of plot and hero development, examining a narrow range of specific story-building tasks: Robert McKee constructs the value progression (the pattern of change in the hero's value orientations), Joseph Campbell identifies the hero's type of reaction to circumstances, Alfred Adler constructs the hero's motives for action, Rollo Rhys May constructs the hero's self-awareness, Erik Erikson examines his identity crisis, and Carl Gustav Jung examines the hero's driving forces and life orientations. Thus, if we combine all the models into a complex integrated structure - the cyclic tetrachotomy - we obtain the following compositional progression:

I. Exposure of the hero: The hero is passive, gullible, unaware of his true abilities, does virtually nothing to change his situation, despite being the bearer of the story's positive value, and as a result of circumstances beyond his control at the time, the hero loses something of particular value to him. At this stage in the story's development, the hero appears as an egocentric individual whose aspirations are geared towards finding ways to satisfy his own needs.

II. Hero's motivation: following the changes brought about by fateful circumstances, the hero is ready to assert his right to autonomy, attempts to free himself from the oppression of circumstances and find the inner strength to fight it, but as he avoids difficult tasks, responsibilities and obligations, he must adapt to the oppression of circumstances, with the result that the hero becomes the bearer of the story's limiting value. At this stage in the story's development, the hero appears as a person oriented towards finding a way out of the situation, seeking to learn and adapt to the new realities of his life.

III. Hero Action: Because of the resentment that builds up.
The hero realizes his potential and achieves an important external goal. The hero is ready to act actively to achieve an important external goal, aspiring to superiority and domination over others, and thus becomes the bearer of the story's negative value. At this stage of the story's development, the hero appears as an active person, acting spontaneously, but with a clear idea of his goals and objectives, and matching the psychological characteristics of his antipode.

IV. The hero's catharsis: following the battle for an important external goal, the hero finds himself in an illusion - that is, the hero is the bearer of an extremely negative value in the story, but because the hero, in his self-awareness, goes beyond the limits of his own personality, he feels the crisis and failure of his worldviews, which encourages him to a desperate but meaningful set of actions aimed at defeating the forces of antagonism. As a result, the antipodean hero, through desperate self-denial, turns to socially useful activity. At this point in the story's development, the hero actively moves from marginal values and worldviews to altruistic values aimed at the good of his fellow man.

The proposed model focuses primarily on the protagonist, i.e. the main character in the story. However, in some pictures, this model is realized not only in the main plot linked to the protagonist, but also in the subplots and related characters. In general, the dramatic (including adventure) hero seems to be highly regulated, although sometimes this regulation is rather implemented in a subtle organization of

CHAPTER 3
MYTHOLOGEMES, MYTHS AND ARCHETYPES IN BELARUSIAN ADVENTURE CINEMA

Belarusian adventure cinema is characterized by pan-European tendencies within the adventure film group, actively resorting to genre synthesis, which, for example, was not characteristic of most genres in the adventure film group of American cinema until the 1990s [50, p. 45]. It is particularly important to note the tendency to introduce comic elements into adventure films, as this characteristic of European and Belarusian adventure cinema constitutes a significant difference from American cinema, which only began to actively introduce comic elements after the success of Hong Kong comic action films on the North American film market [50, p. 162-164]. This trend allows us to conclude that Belarusian adventure cinema, in its genre aspect, has developed in line with European trends, which have always endeavored to "defuse" the serious atmosphere of adventure cinema and the synthesis of genres as a tool to meet audience expectations.

To a large extent, the synthesis of genres in cinema is based on the literary tradition, in which an adventure story is inconceivable without ironic-comic, melodramatic and lyrical lines. What's more, this characteristic of European and Belarusian literature has fairly deep roots, which, in a certain sense, allows us to see it in the context of the use of archetypes and mythologemes that have shaped audience expectations. Confirmation of this idea, which can be described as a thesis - "the spectator himself knows the formulas of all genres", can be found in Dmitry Salynsky's article "Sketches to the Problem of Genres in Cinema" [29]. [29].

Another distinctive feature of Belarusian adventure cinema is the traditional emphasis on military and children's films. Although the group of adventure genres in Belarusian cinema is represented by a rich palette of genres, the most striking examples of adventure genres are associated with children's and youth films, and war films.

As far as adventure films for children and teenagers in Belarus are concerned, we can note that in terms of genre, these films are represented by the fantasy, adventure, detective and science fiction genres.

In the early 1970s, the film "Spring Fairy Tale" hit television screens. It can be classified in the melodramatic fantasy genre, based on the fairy tale "The Snow Maiden" by A.N. Ostrovsky. The "Spring Fairy Tale" is an interpretation of the myth of forbidden love, in which we can find a strongly transformed mythologem of brothers in love with one woman.

The next notable example from this group is the film "Zimorodok", which tells the story of schoolboy Marat's search for an underground hero nicknamed Zimorodok. In this film, the adventure genre is resolved with the help of a detective motif - the search for a war hero by schoolchildren. The film's key archetype is the image of the defender of the people, embodied by the partisan nicknamed Zimorodok. The film's plot is not based on any explicit mythology.

The most striking Soviet film for children and adolescents of the period under consideration is 1973's Kortik. From the point of view of the classical model of the three-act structure, each episode of Kortik is a separate act; meanwhile, this film corresponds to the cyclic tetrachotomy discussed in the second chapter of this thesis. Structurally, the cyclic tetrachotomy of this film appears as an ostinatory progression of the basic plot, whose framework is constituted by the realities of civil war, the mystery contained in the dirk and the just punishment of the criminal in the person of Nikitsky.

The iconography of the painting is based on a fabula built around secret knowledge (known in Slavic folklore as "Go there, I know not where. Bring back I don't know what"), correlated with the myth of Jason and the search for the Golden Fleece (the return of lost valuables from Colchis to his homeland). Furthermore, the main iconographic dominants of the Jason myth echo the symbols incorporated into the film's plot. The very image of the dirk refers to the iconography of the sword, a symbol of bravery, power and administrative justice [38, p. 358]. The image of power is interpreted in the context of the fate of the dirk's owners: power passed from aristocrats to revolutionaries (Polevoy); power was tempted by bandits - the "forces of evil" (Nikitsky); finally, power passed into the hands of the decent younger generation (Misha).

The image of the dirk (symbol of administrative justice),
The bayonet, as an analogue of the sword, is interpreted as one of Melpomene's symbols [38, p. 359]. In addition, the dirk as an analogue of the sword is interpreted as one of Melpomene's symbols [38, P. 359], which is also relevant, given the children's zeal in organizing the children's drama club and raising funds for the starving people of the Volga region through theatrical performances. The watch, which is the main piece of the dirk puzzle, is "an attribute of moderation personified" [38, p. 614]. [It symbolizes the cautious attitude of the Soviet authorities towards newly-acquired wealth, which the dirk kept secret.

"The Bronze Bird" and "The Last Summer of Childhood" (both released in 1974) are sequels to "Kortik". These films reinforce the image of young Soviet adventurers created in Kortik, which explains the structural and compositional homogeneity of these films, which retain the dominance of the mythologem of secret knowledge, but have a more active police component. The mythologem of secret knowledge is characteristic of the films in question (Kortik, L'oiseau de bronze and Le dernier été de l'enfance, except that the latter has a more active detective component).
In particular, the mythology of secret knowledge underpins the plots of the "Indiana Jones" film franchise, "The Da Vinci Code", as well as the successes of the last decade - "The Lord of the Code". In particular, the mythologem of secret knowledge underpins the plots of the "Indiana Jones" film franchise, "The Da Vinci Code", as well as the cinematic successes of the last decade - "The Lord of the Rings", "Harry Potter", "Pirates of the Caribbean", "Arthur and the Invisibles".

Returning to "The Bronze Bird" and "The Last Summer of Childhood", it should be noted that the iconography of the paintings also continues the semantic tradition of "Kortik", replacing the image of the sword with a combination of images of a bird of prey (symbol of strength and victory [38, P. 406]) and a diamond (symbolizing the ephemerality of earthly goods [38, P. 224]), as well as the image of relics as a paraphrase of Navrotsky's documents in "The Last Summer of Childhood".

It's worth noting the specificity of the images' embodiment and the plot's correlation with the mythologemes identified. The events depicted in all three films relate to the formative period of Soviet power, and the main ideological function of Misha and his comrades is to serve as a moral mold for the young builders of communism. In this context, the formalization of certain images becomes understandable, as does the particular static psychological nature of the images of the characters, who cannot overtly manifest a progression of negative values or fully identify with their "shadow". A study of viewer reviews on online forums and web portals (mainly kinopoisk.gtsy kino-teatr.ru) even shows the archetype of Misha Polyakov as a brave fighter for justice in the Soviet pantheon of film heroes, although the hero of Anatoly Rybakov's novels appears as a rather flattened and exaggerated patriotic model of the hero. At the same time, the Soviet neo-mythology of the last two decades of the USSR's existence put not only Misha Polyakov, but also the plot of "Kortik" on a pedestal as the myth of the Soviet patriotic teenager.

"The Adventures of Pinocchio" 1975 is based on the prodigal son archetype, as the whole story of Pinocchio's maturation is almost a direct incarnation of this biblical New Testament myth. The original source of "Pinocchio" - Carlo Collodi's "Pinocchio" - depicts the story of the prodigal son in a manner closer to the original mythology, Pinocchio being more of a prodigal son than Pinocchio. Pinocchio is a modification of the original character, carrying a simple warning message for a children's audience, skipping the difficult stages of Pinocchio's story so that children can interpret it for themselves. Despite the deviations from the basic story, it can be said that the key motifs of the myth and mythology of the prodigal son are present in The Adventures of Pinocchio.

The 1977 film "Little Red Riding Hood" is the second most brilliant example of cinema for children and teenagers after "Kortik". The plot of "Little Red Riding Hood", transposed into the film's screenplay from Charles Perrault's tale, is an interpretation of the French version of a tale widespread in European folklore, about a little girl who meets a wolf. Most folkloric examples of this story have a strong sexual connotation and involve the triumph of the wolf who kills the little girl. Famous literary versions (treatment of the original story by Charles Perrault and the Grimm brothers) tone down the sexual motifs and offer a different ending, in which the little girl manages to save herself. The "Little Red Riding Hood" myth is an ethnopedagogical tale about the danger of strangers and, in a way, correlates with the mythologem of the hypocritical conqueror (through the image of the wolf).

The film "Little Red Riding Hood" departs sharply from the basic plot and is a free interpretation of it, since the film's action takes place after the events described in the fairy tale and is based on the moral attitude of forgiving the old enmity. It's worth noting that the wolf brothers and Little Red Riding Hood both represent the archetypal "fool". The wolves are fools because, without being villains, they agree to take revenge on Little Red Riding Hood. Red Riding Hood is an interpretation of the simple-minded, gullible Ivan the Fool of Russian folklore. Despite the original myth of a young girl who meets a treacherous wolf, and the basic plot of this myth, the original mythological motifs are absent from "About Little Red Riding Hood".

The following example of adventure cinema for children and young people - the 1981 fairy tale "Sold Laughter", based on the novel "Tim Thaler, or Sold Laughter" by writer James Crews, not only corresponds entirely to the quaternary structure of the cyclic tetrachotomy, but is also based on two important archetypes of the Western European situation - the pact with the devil and the devil's deception. Tim Thaler, the film's protagonist, completes a full cycle of psychological development: from the receiver type, bearer of the story's positive value, to the "epiphanic", socially useful, self-sacrificing personality type, moving from a marginal value-bearer to a bearer of the original positive value. In his literary work, Crews establishes moral values that supersede the dominant importance of material well-being, establishing the value of smiles and laughter as the embodiment of human virtues.

To continue the examination of domestic adventure films for children and teenagers and the incorporation of mythologemes into these films, it's worth looking at the sci-fi comedy film Summer Impressions on Planet Z (1986), a perestroika parody of Spielberg's Alien (based on the work by William Kotzwinkle). Felix, who has arrived from Planet X, corresponds to Spielberg's I.P. in his importance to the Earthlings who have taken him in, hiding him from outsiders (mainly from the main antagonist, the barber-sorcerer Mihalych). In practical terms, as with I.P., the alien Felix's return home is linked to his escape from terrestrial life.

of the malevolent. However, the similarity between I.P. and Felix is extremely conditional, as Felix Lucky appears as the archetypal "bishop of fools". The alien boy asks questions with obvious answers, or reports information to the spaceship in the categories of an idealistic philosopher, although the film's authors intended him to be the Little Prince in a new way. Exupéry's Little Prince is an example of a pure, childlike, yet mature soul, while Felix Lucky, scripted by Yuri Tomin and directed by E. Markovsky, is more a child of his age, burdened with no experience except the existential categories of extraterrestrial intelligence.

This image is perhaps the only one of the juvenile strips that does not correspond to the cyclical tetrachotomy: the progression of values has only a limited, positive value (indifference and friendship). Felix's evolution is formal, and consists in the fact that, being a humanoid thinking matter at the beginning of the story, Felix acquires certain human traits. However, Felix remains a kind of golem (created not from clay by the Orthodox Jews of Prague, but from flesh and blood and extraterrestrial beings). Felix's main evolution is the attempt to transform himself from a golem into an ordinary boy. Only the physics teacher, a constant bearer of positive values, is the source of coherent psychological evolution.

The film is also notable for its scathing satire of avant-garde art, realized through the image of the rock ensemble "Astronauts". The film's director depicts the musical group as a collection of extremely unserious, infantile young people who overestimate the extent of their talent. The apotheosis of this caricature of "high" art is the rock opera "14 Floors of Solitude", directed by the leader of the "Astronauts", Andrew Morkovkin. Analysis of this work by the film industry in Soviet Belarus shows that the "perestroika fever" in society was also reflected in the cinema. This led to the creation of a "mixed film" of The Little Prince, Alien and the legend of the Golem of Prague, spiced up with the passions of espionage and the aesthetics of buffoonery. However, the film is a true mirror of the worldview of teenagers in the perestroika era, which mixed noble moral principles with a confused desire for creative expression.

The late 1980s saw the children's adventure films Flight into Monsterland (1986), based on the myth of the Messiah (thanks to which the motifs of the nation's savior mythos can be discerned in the film), and Peter Pan (1987), based, like its literary source, on a modified myth of the prodigal son (indicating the presence of the corresponding mythos).

The development of the adventure genre for children and young people came to a standstill for a long time after the collapse of the USSR: the last decade of the 20th century was marked by an almost total absence of Belarusian adventure films for children and teenagers. It was not until the beginning of the 21st century that Belarusian film production resurrected the adventure genre for a younger audience.

The return of the adventure genre to the screen for children and young people is associated with Elena Turova's New Year's Adventures in July (2008), based on the mythological image of the nation's defender, Sasha and Dasha defending Earth's vacations against a xenomorph invader - the evil G ala virus.

The most brilliant adventure film for children and teenagers of the first decade of the 21st century can be described as "Carrot in the Mirror", directed in 2010 by Elena Turova. The prehistory of the main plot - the struggle of twin brothers Morris and Sebastian for the hand of the beautiful Mona, played by Alesa Samokhovets, embodies the mythology of brothers in love with the same woman (the jealous villain who doesn't get his beloved destroys the rival). The main character of the girl Veronica, who is the offspring of the fairy-tale monarch, is presented as a paraphrase of the mythological image of the nation's protector, resolved through the biblical myth of Moses. According to the fairy-tale version of the story, it was Gennady Ivanovich who discovered Bibilus, under whose guise he hides,
the girl was carried into the real world by a stork in a basket, just as in the biblical myth of Moses, where a mother sends her child across the waters of the Nile in a basket of reeds. Like Moses, Veronica, when she learned she was dead, was transported in a basket.
The Egyptian, who no longer has a destiny, goes to the evil Mortis, the former Prince Morris, to get him to let his people go. It's true that the "seven plagues of Egypt" are

not carried out by "the evil one".
Pharaoh" Mortis, and Veronica herself, to find the coveted book, an artifact capable of destroying the evil magician. The parallel is also suggested by the solution to Mortis' death, which is similar to that of the Pharaoh: both are buried in the abyss thanks to the intervention of supernatural forces. In the case of the Pharaoh, the abyss is the waters of the Red Sea, and in the case of Mortis, it is the ceilings of the ancient library. The free interpretation of the mythological source is reflected in the "simplification" of the protagonist's image. If Veronica had suffered the temptation to be close to her father (there is no father in the real world, nor in the world of fairy tales), passing for a time to the "dark side" and asserting a marginal value, her image would have been more complete and authentic.

As far as the theme of value progression is concerned, it's worth noting the image's partial correspondence with cyclic tetrachotomy, since the inconsistency with the four-step development proposed for the hero's archetypal states lies in the inconsistency between value progression and hero typology. As far as typology is concerned. Veronica appears from the outset as an active type of hero, evolving towards a hyperactive type. The value embodied by the protagonist remains permanently positive - the hegemony of goodness. In addition, the plot of the picture corresponds to the asserted model of the mythologem. Thus, the motivating factor at the beginning is Veronica herself ("persona"), then appears Bibilus ("wise old man"), then Mortis ("shadow") and at the end - Alesya - Veronica's mother ("anima"). The heroine's orientation also passes through the four stages proposed: her own person (Veronica is a princess), understanding the conjuncture (Veronica has Nedalia's fate in her hands), destroying the antagonist (ridding the peoples of fairyland of the evil sorcerer) and the good of loved ones and society (saving her mother, the silkworms, the fairy world and the real world), which corresponds to the progression of the heroine's motivations: Veronica appears as a receiving type, then as an avoiding type, then as a controlling type, and finally as a socially useful type. The controlling characteristic of the heroine is also in four stages: inferiority (Veronica has no father), humility (the little girl has been given a role inappropriate for her age), desperation (pursuing the silk book) and self-sacrifice (Veronica abandons the book to save her mothers, both from the real world and the world of fairy tales), which also perfectly illustrates the progression of psychological archetypes: Veronica passes through the stases of "orphan", "wanderer", "warrior" and "martyr". The same applies to the heroine's self-awareness: innocence (Veronica is the daughter of a librarian), rebellion (Veronica's challenging perception of the new reality), ordinary (Veronica accepts her noble origin and realizes her ability to fight Mortis), creative (Veronica finds a way to triumph over the antagonist). The driving force of "Carrot" also alternates between four states: naiveté (not understanding the magnitude of the antagonist), protest (identifying the forces of antagonism), external objective (destroying Mortis) and high objective (saving her mother). The girl's existential crisis also unfolds in four phases: identity passes through the stages of confidence and distrust, autonomy and doubt, initiative and guilt, and Veronica's development ends with the identity crisis of diligence and inferiority.

The relatively cool perception of part of the audience of "The Carrot in the Mirror", based on a comparison of this film with its foreign counterparts released on the domestic film distribution market, highlights the film's only major drawback. If we omit the caricature of the passing characters, such as library director Vadim Vygovorevich or, for example, the mischievous virus Chyukh, because in children's and youth films, caricatured passing characters are part of the genre convention, we can't omit the caricature of the antagonist.

Foreign adventure films for children and teenagers feature a complex, multi-dimensional villain as their antagonist. In "Harry Potter", "The Chronicles of Narnia" and "Arthur and the Minims", the antagonist is a repugnant villain (Lord Voldemort, the Witch and the Horrible Urdalak respectively), who is not, however, devoid of attractive qualities, as his official story resembles a struggle for justice. The "seductive villain"'s acquisition of unlimited power is a matter of honor, since, according to him, power was illegally taken from him, and he himself is an unfortunate outcast who has been oppressed by the "forces of good". In the objective reality of the story, the story of the "seductive villain" that he is an unfortunate victim of the terrible and cruel bias of the protagonist's forces is in fact a lie, but the spectator must sympathize with the villain for a short while, especially if, in order to destroy the hero, the villain pretends to be a repentant "lost sheep" ready to take the path of truth. Without the antagonist passing through the archetypal "wolf in sheep's clothing" stage, where his feint is the last available means of defeating the protagonist, Mortis' image in "Carrot" is greatly simplified, even if his bitterness and imperial ways have an explanation (his love has been rejected by the princess, who has preferred him to her twin brother). But why Mortis decides to move from the fairy-tale world to the real world is unclear. The image of a seductive villain in foreign films is based on the mythology of the hypocritical conqueror. Mortis, on the other hand, is a singular archetype of the evil genius.

The last adventure film for children and teenagers released on the Belarusian screen was The Incredible Displacement (2014). The film tells the story of Vanya Fedorov's correction of a violation of the space-time continuum. The film has no explicit basis in the form of a mythology underlying the plot.

Another important sub-genre of Belarusian adventure cinema is the heroic-adventure genre. The most brilliant film of this genre in the 1970s was the TV series Ruins Shoot at Point Blank Range (1970), 47

The film tells the story of the heroic activities of Minsk's anti-fascist resistance during the Nazi occupation of the Belarusian capital. In a sense, the film embodies the mythology of the defender of the nation, but as the plot is mainly based on the real-life stories of Minsk's underground fighters, this mythology is not particularly vivid.

If we consider the group of adventure films in Belarusian cinematography of the following decade, we should mention the historical heroic adventure series "State Border". Eight series were released during the decade under review: "We are ours, we are new..." (1980), "The Peaceful Summer of the 21st Year". (1980), "Eastern Frontier" (1982), "Red Sand" (1984), "Year Forty-First" (1986), "Beyond the Threshold of Victory" (1987), "Salt Wind" (1988), "On the Far Frontier" (1988).

In the film "We are ours, we are new", the mythology of the prodigal son is realized. Vladimir, the protagonist, undergoes an evolution that conforms to the cyclical tetrachotomy model. He goes from being a tsarist border guard officer (= orphan), a stranger to the new Soviet Russia, ready to go abroad and leave his homeland forever (= vagabond), preventing mass unrest on the Dvinsk border (= warrior), to a patriot (= martyr) who breaks off relations with his mother for the sake of his homeland. The central archetype, not only in We Are Ours, We Are New, but also in subsequent films in the State Border series, is the image of the fatherland.

The sixth film in the series, "Beyond the Threshold of Victory", moves into the detective genre for the first time. In this film, the main action unfolds according to the canons of the spy thriller genre.

The main character, Andrei, sent to the Banderite camp in the post-war years, is the archetypal Trojan horse. The image of Christina, Andrei's fiancée, who comes to her father's farm and finds herself at the mercy of the Banderites, corresponds to the image of Soviet Ukraine, which, like Christina, finds itself at the mercy of bandits. The actions of the combined heroes correspond to the progression of psychological archetypes as motivating factors: "Persona" (Andrei the border guard), "Teacher" (the teacher), "Bander" (the man) and "Bander" (the man).
(a general), "Shadow" (Andrei in the guise of a Banderovite) and "Anima" (Christina). The film's plot corresponds entirely to the cyclical tetrachotomy model. The hero passes through all the developmental stages of this model. The film is based on the modernized mythology of the defender of the nation.

The model for the last three films in the "State Border" cycle - the male and female leads are presented as a border guard and his beloved with a "tarnished reputation". Thus, Andrei's mistress Christina is the sister of a Banderovite's mistress; Belov Sr.'s wife is the daughter of a Nazi criminal; Belov Jr.'s mistress is the former wife of an engineer recruited by the foreign secret service.

The most brilliant film in Belarusian post-Soviet cinema is M. Ptashuk's "In August '44". The film's plot is based on Captain Alekhine's group's search for saboteurs with the call sign "K.O.", and is not clearly influenced by mythology. The evolution of the protagonist (Captain Alekhine) generally corresponds to cyclic tetrachotomy, with the exception of the progression of the motivating factor and motives, which is generally characteristic of detective films. The progression of values is based on the transformation of the initial positive value of truth (in the context of the disclosure of residence at the rear of both Red Army fronts). The limiting value of partiality/doubt is realized in Alekhine's uncertainty about the composition of the subversive group. The negative value of illusion is embodied in a false lead in the search for the group marked "K.O." (Captain Nikolaev and Lieutenant Sentsov). The marginal value is linked to the confrontation with the troops' superiors (acting before a major troop operation in the Shilovichi forest). The progression of control properties also corresponds to the cyclical tetrachotomy: the death of Leshka Basos (deficiency/"orphan"), the investigation by a small group (humility/"vagabond"), the development of a false lead and the fact that suspect Pavlovsky shot himself (despair/"warrior"), the operation in the Shilovichi forest and the threat of a tribunal (self-sacrifice/"martyr").

The film "In August '44", based on the work of the same name by V. Bogomolov, has no obvious mythological basis, but there are elements of the medieval myth of a knight playing chess with death. The presence of this myth is rather conventional and is reflected in the hero's attitude to the investigation. Alekhine risks being court-martialed (in the case of the failure of the Neman operation) or killed (in the case of the arrest of a group of saboteurs), just like the knight of the myth who risks either dying himself, or giving death to a loved one.

The film's main archetype is that of the forest, a sacred and dangerous place for man. The film's characters are associated with the archetypes of the skeptic (Blinov), the faithful squire (Evgeny) and the devil's trickster (Alekhin). Despite the correlation between August '44 and cyclic tetrachotomy, as well as the fact that the archetypes and motifs mentioned from the myth of the knight (playing with death) can be found in the film, there is no obvious influence of mythologemes on the plot of this film.

Post-Soviet Belarusian heroic adventure cinema has relatively little to do with mythologizing. The main films of this period are You're on a Mission (2004), The Shield of the Fatherland (2007) and In June 1941 (2008).

The adventure genre was also present in Belarusian adventure cinema. A typical example of this genre is the film "Time-Not-Waiting" (1975), which corresponds perfectly to the cyclic tetrachotomy, as well as to the social archetype of the Klondike nouveau riche at the time of the gold rush at the turn of the 19th and 20th centuries, and to the mythologem of the prodigal son. There can be no doubt that such a far-reaching extrapolation of the mythologem rests on the basic material, namely the work of Jack London, who was characterized by the creation of universal hero images in his books, constructing characters based on his own life experience, which reflected many cultural and mythological archetypes.

In many ways, Time-Not-Waiting is very similar to the aforementioned Sold Laughter. It's extremely clear that the foreign literary material reflects Christian cultural dominants: Elam Harnish and Tim Thaler are characters who disseminate the vision of material wealth as the embodiment of marginal value, which points back to the primary source of this type of story - the myth of the "prodigal son" [38, P. 107] - the traditional basis of maturation/re-education stories the myth of the "prodigal son" [38, P. 107] - the traditional basis of maturation/re-education stories. Elam, like the prodigal son, leaves his native land for wealth, but like the prodigal son, Harnish is forced to return to the starting point, having lost everything. Tim Thaler is a slightly more complex "prodigal son", for Tim's "abandoned home" (the archetype of true value) is his smile and laughter, which he also sells for material wealth - the gift of winning all bets. Tim the "prodigal son" doesn't lose his material fortune, he loses himself by alienating those dear to him, forcing him to reinvent himself and find ways to "bring the prodigal son home" by deceiving the infernal antagonist, turning his disadvantage to his advantage.

Other important components of the adventure genre group - the detective and thriller genres in Belarussian cinema of the period under consideration - are peculiar and curious. The liveliest crime film of the 70s - King Stakh's Wild Hunt (1979) directed by V. Rubinchik - refers in part to the mythology of the seal of Cain (as an ancestral curse). However, the peculiarity of V. Korotkevich's material, which constructs the plot of his story as a typical thriller, where all the mystical phenomena at first glance turn out to be Dubotovka's insidious intention to drive Nadezhda to madness, has leveled this mythologem. It is this characteristic of crime thrillers, when the original supernatural nature of the event, which refers the viewer to mythologemes (realized in legends and mystical myths), is revealed as a carefully planned criminal plot, which refutes the influence of the original mythologemes. Korotkevich describes this genre-specific attitude towards mystical prejudice with Nadezhda's words: "Legends are filth generated by the minds of savages".

The image of the Bolotnye Yaliny estate, created by the authors of the painting, combined with E. Glebov's music, creates a genre noir atmosphere, incorporating the main archetype of the painting - the swamp archetype. In traditional Belarusian culture, the swamp is the abode of infernal forces. It is home to the main representatives of the impure pantheon of Belarusian folklore: lutsypar, shaton and bognik. The swamp is also a symbol of stagnation and decomposition.

Ethnographer Beloretsky is the archetypal Messiah. The coming of the Messiah is preceded by a prophecy which, in King Stach's Wild Hunt, is the presentation of the Batlake. By analyzing the correlation between the Messiah archetype and the film's protagonist, we can also note the following coincidence: the Messiah sacrifices himself to defeat the forces of evil, which is what happens to Beloretsky, who is arrested by the tsar's gendarmerie for organizing a popular revolt. The day on which the story ends is also symbolic: January 1, 1901, the first day of the new twentieth century, marking the arrival of a new era.

It's worth noting that the plot of this thriller revolves around the European mythology of the ancestral curses of noble families. Traditionally, these myths are based either on the mythology of the seal of Cain, or on the mythology of fate (destiny, inevitable fate). However, as we saw above, due to the detective nature of the genre, myth in its traditional form breaks down, as do the mythologems on which these myths are based. The plot is filled with the living archetypes of the martyr, the madman, the victim and the damned.

"Black Castle Olshansky" (1984, directed by M. Ptashuk) is another example of the detective genre, linking the realities of different historical eras. As in most treasure hunter stories, traces of the presence of the mythologism of secret knowledge can be seen in the film: the key to the mystery is the Gospel of 1534, the antagonist who keeps the secret betrays his existence by killing Maryan, Cosmich finds hidden in the spine of 52

He manages to investigate the mystery thanks to the young archaeologist Stanislava Rechits. Olshansky's Black Castle" is very close to the mythologem mentioned, but due to the canons of the detective genre, this mythologem is very much transformed.

Olshansky's Black Castle is based on the archetype of inevitable punishment, present both in the main detective story and in the retrospective flashes of Anton Kosmic's consciousness (in which he sees himself as Valiuzhinich - the leader of a popular uprising). The picture corresponds almost entirely to the cyclical tetrachotomy, with the exception of the stimulus, which contains the four stages described, but in a different order (the sequences "persona, old sage, anima, shadow" instead of "persona, old sage, shadow, anima").

The progression of values passes through four stages of development: truth (positive), indifference (borderline), illusion (negative) and negation of the presence of truth (marginal). The change in governing properties also corresponds to the cyclical tetrachotomy: damage (loss of a friend), humility (recognition of the existence of a three-hundred-year-old secret), despair (active search for the treasure) and self-sacrifice (risking one's own life to reveal the doctor's true identity).

The next example of a crime film is the 2013 mini-series "Traces of the Apostles", which looks like a new interpretation of "Olshansky's Black Castle". The story is built within the polysyuzhet framework: two independent lines are present - each with its own genre characteristics and narrative logic. The modern plot of Alevtina (a trainee who has arrived in Niasvizh to practice her profession in the investigation department) is built according to the canons of the classic English detective genre: an atypical detective (Alevtina), a devious assistant (Grigory), a boring policeman (Viktor), an unobvious villain (Bronevitsky). The plot takes place in 1942 (the expedition to Nesvizh of Soviet spy Henry, who hides under the guise of 53 years old).

This book is an example of a spy detective in the spirit of Bogomil Raynov's works.

Despite the eclecticism of "Traces of the Apostles", a transformed mythology of secret knowledge can be found in the film: the motive for the crime for Alevtina, the secret laboratory for Heinrich and the sculptures of the apostles for Wagner. We'd like to pay particular attention to the character of Professor Otto Wagner. Wagner, who is behind the expedition, is presented as a typical occultist, whose main task is to gather thirteen pieces of a meteorite, divided by Genghis Khan, with the aim of world domination, reflecting the mythologem of a hypocritical conqueror. Wagner is a typical multidimensional "charming villain", which makes his character interesting for the viewer and, together with Igor Sigov's acting work, constitutes one of the film's strongest images. However, it's also worth noting that, as befits a spy detective, Wagner is not the real antagonist, but Soviet intelligence agent Vogel, who was recruited by German counter-intelligence, i.e. a traitor on his own side.

When it comes to the adventure genre in Belarusian cinema, we can't fail to mention the national action films. The most prominent representatives of this genre are The Nuclear Zone Ranger (1999), as well as Sniper: Weapon of Vengeance (2001) and Lethal Combat (2010), which actively interact with the spy thriller and detective genres.

"Ranger from the Atomic Zone" not only belongs to the action film genre, but is also a typical example of the western genre. The only difference with the classic western is that the action of "Ranger" takes place in the era of the "dashing nineties". The exclusion zone corresponds ideologically to the Wild West, with its dashing mores and anarchy.

("A state within a state", as one local fisherman puts it).

radiation contamination). Captain Second Rank Alexey Barsuk is the absolute embodiment of the cowboy archetype. It's also worth noting that the "cowboy" 54 Badger has a trusty horse (a gray LuAZ 969M all-terrain vehicle) and a revolver (a large-caliber rifle) to intimidate his enemies. The antagonist Vitalik is also a typical Western bandit ("bad cowboy"). The young girl Vika embodies the image of a western bandit's beautiful friend (the girl suffers from a relationship with the bandit and feels attracted to the cowboy). All this allows us to consider "The Ranger from the Atomic Zone" as an incarnation of the North American myth of the noble cowboy who returns home to a provincial Wild West town suffering from the arbitrariness of bandits.

Badger's controlling property and psychological archetype correspond to the cyclical tetrachotomy: a downsized naval officer (inferiority/"orphan"), a forester adapting to the realities of the alienation zone (humility/"vagabond"), a guardian of order fighting delinquents (despair/"warrior"), a liquidator of a criminal group saving his beloved (self-sacrifice/"martyr"). The progression of motivations also develops according to the asserted pattern: to receive (starting a new life after divorce), to avoid (not confronting delinquents), to control (gaining the upper hand over delinquents),
At first, he's passive, then inactive, then active, then active, and by the end of the story, he's hyperactive. In the beginning, he's passive, then inactive, then active, and by the end of the story, he's hyperactive. The hero's self-awareness and driving force also pass through four stages of development: innocence/naiveté (ignorance of what's happening in the exclusion zone), rebellion/protest (protest against the bandits' arbitrary behavior), ordinary self-awareness/external purpose (understanding his role and destroying Vitalik's criminal network), creative self-awareness/higher purpose (understanding that only the hero himself can destroy the antagonist, and save Vicky from the bandits). Cyclic tetrachotomy corresponds to the hero's orientation and motivating factor: his own persona (a retired divorced military officer), understanding of the situation/"wise old man" (his 55-year-old father), and the "wise old man" (his father).
the destruction of the antagonist/"shadow" (Vitalik), the good of loved ones/"anima" (saving Vicky).

Value progression and identity change depart from the cyclical tetrachotomy model. The progression of values is divided between the permanent value of justice, which is at the heart of the story, and the contextual value of a peaceful "new life". The contextual value of the protagonist's development passes through four characteristic stages: positive, limiting, negative and marginal. However, since the main value of the story remains permanent, it can be argued that the progression of

values in the picture deviates from the cyclical tetrachotomy model. The same applies to Badger's identity. The protagonist's identity is constructed according to the progression "autonomy vs. doubt, diligence vs. inferiority, initiative vs. guilt" instead of the progression "trust/distrust, autonomy/doubt",
initiative/guilt, diligence/inferiority".

From the point of view of the mythological underpinnings of the plot of "The Atomic Zone Ranger", the motifs of the mythologem of the guardian of the world of the dead, whose task is to protect the two worlds from interaction (the guardian must not allow the living to enter the world of the dead and must protect the world of the living from the dangerous inhabitants of the world of the dead) can be traced. However, despite the second-rate captain's ideological correlation with the mythologism of the guardian of the underworld, this mythologism is not structuring for the film in question, due to the dominance of the acute element of plot and western mythology.

Foreign cinema of the adventure genre cannot be imagined without horror films. The only example of a horror film in domestic cinema is A. Kudinenko's "Masakra" (2010), based on Prosper Merimee's short story "Lokis". In the context of this story, we can consider the myth of the werebear. The werebear is a widespread image in Germanic, Scandinavian, Finno-Ugric and Celtic cultures, as well as in other national cultures that have interacted with them. The bear archetype, which is the key to this myth, comes from one of the fetish animals of Indo-European culture, transformed in Scandinavian culture into an aggressive berserker (berserk). In domestic culture, the shapeshifting bear is often a person (or the descendant of such a person) punished for cruelty or evil deeds, which allows us to read the plot of this painting as an interpretation of the myth of an ancestral curse. It's difficult to trace a specific mythologem in this situation, as the mythology of ancestral curses emerged as a class prejudice (explaining the nobility's closure to marriages with commoners), which explains the disparity in the basic plots of these works.

The protagonist of "Masakra" - the adventurer Nikolai Kazantsev, who pretends to be a scientist in order to realize his dream of studying art in Italy - corresponds in many ways to the cyclic tetrachotomy. The inciting factors pass through four stages of

development: the "persona" (Nikolai dreaming of Italy), the "wise old man" (Father Paul instructing Nikolai), the "shadow" (Count Vladimir Pazurkevich "stealing" Nikolai's beloved), the "anima" (Anna). Control properties and psychological archetypes also correspond to the organizational model of the hero in question: the expelled student
(imperfect/"orphan"), cataloguing the count's library "privy docent" (humble/"vagabond"), preparing a love runaway
(despair/"warrior"), Anna's savior who risks his life (self-sacrifice/"martyr"). The hero's motive, self-awareness, driving force, identity and direction also evolve according to the cyclical tetrachotomy. The divergence is summed up in the progression of values. In "Masakra", the values change four times, but do not form a progression. The table of values in "Masakra" is as follows: positive value of love, positive value of realizing personal dreams, positive value of love, negative value of abandoning personal dreams.

We should also mention several films from Belarusian independent cinema in recent years, which belong to the adventure film genre: "Half-Life" and "Skhvatka".

The plot of the film "Skhvatka" directed by I.Maslyukov (2014) is based on the rivalry between two teams ("Veschiye Olg" and "Maximus") of a popular nighttime urban search game in the first decade of the 21st century. The leader of "Veshchykh Olg" is in love with the leader of "Maximusov", but due to her nefarious character and megalomania, she puts members of both teams at mortal risk, as her main and only goal is to win the "Scramble" at all costs. "Scramble" is an extremely controversial and contradictory strip, whose plot and character motivations can only be understood by an avid player of this game of research. The plot itself is based solely on the value of winning the game, which even affects the parallel melodramatic line with Natasha (Natasha is a lazutnik "prophetic Olga"). The characters resemble simplified casts of modern Belarusian "golden youth" and arouse irritation rather than empathy. Some mythological traits of the eternal rivalry image can be found, which, given the extremely weak work of the screenwriter, is most likely a coincidence.

Director Darya Zhuk's sixteen-minute short Half-Life (2011, co-produced between the USA and Belarus), billed as an adventure drama, is a curious misadventure. In fact, it's an ordinary domestic drama. Michael Pitch and Justin Lieberman's screenplay reflects the utter ignorance of Belarus. On the whole, however, the interest shown by American filmmakers of Belarussian origin gives us hope for the development of creative cooperation in Belarussian film production, as well as the creation of adventure films in their own right.

To summarize the analysis of the influence of mythologemes, myths and archetypes on the adventure genre in Belarusian cinema, the following should be noted:

1. Belarusian adventure cinema is influenced by mythology, myths and archetypes, mainly in adventure and children's films.

2. The universal archetypes found in Belarusian adventure cinema are quite varied; the main archetypes representing the key symbols of the semantic series of images are the national archetypes of the homeland, the land, the forest and the swamp.

3. Cyclic tetrachotomy is used in practically all Belarusian films examined during the Soviet period, with the exception of "Summer Impressions from Planet Z" and crime films.

4. The plots of the films examined tend to use the mythologies of secret knowledge, the prodigal son and the protector of the nation.

CONCLUSION

The key to the structure of works of art is traditionally the hero image, which is not only the principal means of realizing the intention of the author, director and scriptwriter, but also a "mirror" of the public's life and worldview. The search for hero images is always linked to the search for the most comprehensible way for the viewer to reflect the social, political, cultural and spiritual life of modern society, resulting in the creation of heroes and events with a clear and distinct semantics based on the archetypes and mythological experience of society.

The question of the influence of myths and archetypes on cinema is a popular one, and numerous studies have been devoted to it, covering the problem from the angle of different levels of influence on film plots. The problem of mythology, closely related to that of archetypes and myths, has received much less attention.

Mythologem is a category that designates a certain basic fabula, a sequence of archetypes that determines the direction of plot development. In the context of cinema, mythologemes echo the meaning and understanding of philology, anthropology and philosophy as a primordial compositional structure. The integration of mythologemes is rarely conscious, with the exception of the most famous Hollywood examples of the adventure genre (filmmakers such as George Lucas, Steven Spielberg, Jerry Bruckheimer, Luc Besson and others have consciously based their films on mythologemes). The unconscious use of mythologemes is largely based on the screenwriter's translation of his or her cultural and social experience, as well as on the screenwriter's use of his or her intellectual "baggage". The basis for the integration of mythologemes into cinema is cyclic tetrachotomy (changes in the hero's states, identity and worldview).

The influence of mythologemes on cinema is most evident in commercial cinema, which leads us to hypothesize that one of the reasons mythologemes are so present in cinema is that they are not always well represented.

Commercially successful films are mythologems that appeal to the viewer's cultural experience. The most commercially successful films are those of the adventure genre, which indicates that they are more comprehensible to the audience and gives reason to consider this genre group as the most likely to be influenced by mythologems. Indeed, the influence of mythologemes in adventure films is very significant, particularly in American and Western European films. Belarusian adventure films generally conform to European trends in integrating myths into the plot. Moreover, in Belarusian cinema, myths are interpreted according to the specificities of national culture. Thus, in Belarusian adventure films of the Soviet period, three main myths influence the plot of the work itself: secret knowledge, the prodigal son and the protector of the nation.

The proposals in favour of this thesis are supported as follows:

1. Mythologemes, myths and archetypes have had a significant influence on the adventure film genre.

Adventure cinema, the genre most sought-after by audiences the world over, has always been characterized by the strong influence of mythological motifs, archetypes and mythologies in its plots.

The myths common to the adventure film genre are quite numerous. As myths interact with cinema, they are often heavily modified (the myths' original basic fabulae - their mythologemes - are altered).

Mythologemes, in relation to the story being told, are like musical harmony. The vast majority of people associate a particular musical composition with a melody, but the basis of a musical composition is its harmony. Similarly, mythologems are the "harmonies" of story development. As in music, where harmony is the sequence of chords, mythologemes are the sequence of archetypes. Once again, as in the same 61 Many different melodies can be written to the same musical harmony, and many independent stories can be built from the same mythologem.

Adventure films are the embodiment of the average viewer's dream of an adventurous experience involving risk and danger. In order to satisfy this dream, mythologemes are present in these films, as they are the accumulated experience of generations of basic fabulae, which the viewer expects to see embodied on screen. The same applies to archetypes, which are the basic types of characters, heroes and situations.

2. Belarusian adventure cinema is in line with global trends, using the same

archetypal sequences as foreign films of the same genre.

On the basis of the analysis carried out in this thesis, it can be said that adventure films in Belarusian and foreign cinema are similarly influenced by mythologems. In domestic cinema, the plots are based on the mythologies of secret knowledge (treasure-hunting plots), the prodigal son (maturation/re-education plots) and the protector of the nation (plots of struggle against the forces of universal evil), which are familiar to foreign cinema. The mythologies of the brothers in love with the same woman (love triangle), the hypocritical conqueror (main villain) and the apocalypse (fate of the world in the event of the victory of universal evil) are incorporated into the secondary lines.

3. Cyclic tetrachotomy is performed in four parts

The psychological organization of the hero image is the main mechanism for analyzing the presence of mythologemes in cinema.

This four-stage mythology model describes the hero's value attitudes, control property, psychological archetype, motive, self-awareness, driving force, identity, orientation, motivating factor and characterization type of activity during his progressive development, which includes four obligatory stages for each criterion. Such a change in the hero's psychological archetypes (each category is an archetype of the psyche or perception) is widely represented in the works of Western commercial cinema. Cyclic tetrachotomy is also present in domestic films, although in some Belarusian films this pattern is not fully revealed or is totally absent. Based on the idea that the heroes of commercial films are the most comprehensible to their vast target audience, and observing that cyclic tetrachotomy is mainly characteristic of commercial films based on mythologemes, we can hypothesize that this multi-component pattern of four successive changes in the hero's states is key to the viewer's perception, as he or she obviously expects exactly this type of hero evolution.

Summing up the research carried out as part of this Master's thesis, it is possible to note the achievement of the set tasks:

1. The main mythologemes, archetypes and myths that influence the composition of adventure film scripts are identified.

2. Models of mythologemes as basic fabulae of adventure cinema are

explored in the second and third chapters of this master's thesis.

3. The influence of myths on adventure cinema has been studied. The influence of ancient and medieval European myths is most notable. The influence of archetypes on the group of adventure films was studied. The film characters illustrate the following archetypes: "Our acquaintances", "The outsiders", "Lost souls" and "Idols". The archetypes, as types of situation or types of hero's reaction to a situation, are most often manifested in motifs such as bargaining with the devil, bargaining with conscience, sacrifice for salvation, deceiving the devil, etc.

4. The mechanisms by which mythologems influence adventure cinema are characterized, as their own spiritual, cultural, social and intellectual experience is conveyed by the filmmakers.

5. Specific features of the mythologems used in Belarusian adventure cinema are revealed: the tendency to modify mythologems (replacing certain elements of the basic plot with their own interpretations), as well as the use of a small number of original mythologems (the secret knowledge, the prodigal son and the protector of the nation) are highlighted.

The results of this master's thesis are likely to be used in training programs for screenwriters and as a methodology for scriptwriting in genre adventure cinema.

LIST OF SOURCES USED

1. Adler, A. Science of character. Understanding the nature of man / A. Adler. - Moscow: Academic Project, 2014. - 243 c.

2. Aristotle. Poetics. Rhetoric (m) / Aristotle. - M.: Azbuka: Azbuka Klassika. Non-Fiction, 2014. - 320 c.

3. Artemyeva, O. When heroes pass into eternity / O. Artemyeva
[Access mode :
http://www.kinozapiski.rU/ru/article/sendvalues/3/Дата consulted : 22.02.2015

4. Batueva, A. A. Mythologeme of good and evil in the Indo-European languages : author's abstract of the dissertation for the degree of Candidate of Philological Sciences : 10.02.20 / A. A. Batueva ; Military University of the Ministry of Defense of the Russian Federation. - M. , 2008. - 20 c.

5. Bergen, R. Cinema : a guide to genres / R. Bergen. - M.: Kladez-Books, 2011. - 159 c.

6. Vdovushkina, N. S., The archetypal bases of culture at the turn of the XXXXI century. The archetypal bases of culture at the turn of the XXXXI century: thesis author's abstract for the candidate in cultural studies: 24.00.01 / N. S. Vdovushkina ; Saratov State Univ. N. G. Chernyshevsky. - Saratov, 2012. - 22 c.

7. Vodenko, M. O. Interaction of hero and space in modern cinematographic drama: summary of thesis by art history candidate: 17.00.03 / V. M. Olegovna; All-Russian State Institute of Cinematography named after S. A. Gerasimov. S. A. Gerasimov. - M. , 2000. - 30 c.

8. Goran, V. P., Ancient Greek mythologem of fate / Ed. by V. N. Karpovich ; USSR Academy of Sciences, Siberian Branch, Institute of History, Philology and Philosophy. V. N. Karpovich ; USSR Academy of Sciences, Siberian Branch, Institute of History, Philology and Philosophy. - Novosibirsk: Nauka. Siberian Branch, 1990. - 330, c.

9. Gornitskaya, L. I. Mythologem of the island in Russian literature: genesis,

structure, semantics: author's abstract of doctoral dissertation in philological sciences: 10.01.01 / L. I. Gornitskaya ; Southern Federal University. - Volgograd, 2012. - 18 c.

10. Guluk, L. A. Mythologeme of femininity in the culture of the Silver Age : author's abstract of the thesis for the degree of Candidate of Philosophy : 24.00.01 / L. A. Guluk ; Belgorod State University. - Belgorod, 2007. - 19 c.

11. Danilin, A. "Brilliantovaya Rukha", "Kurochka Pryaba" and the Russian Dream. A psychiatrist's free reflections on a favorite movie. [Access mode: http://www.kinozapiski.ru/ru/article/sendvalues/1025/Дата access : 01.03.2015

12. Deleuze, J. Cinéma / J. Deleuze. - M.: Ad Marginem, 2004. - 624 c.

13. Genres of cinema : collection of scientific articles / Research Institute of Theory and History of Cinema ; ed. by V.I.Fomin. - Moscow : Art, 1979. - 319 c.

14. Zaitseva, L. All Belarusian films. T. 2: Cinéma de jeu (1971-1983): catalogue-guide: catalogue-guide. Cinéma de jeux, 1971-1983 /И. Avdeev, L. Zaitseva; scientific editor A. Krasinski. - Minsk: Bel. nauvuka, 2000. - 298 c.

15. Izvorska-Elizarieva, M. N. Myth. Music. Mozart. "Magic Flute" - cosmogonic mythologeme: written by M. N. Izvorska-Elizarieva; Belarus National Academy of Sciences, Institute of Philosophy and Law. - Minsk, 1999. - 33 c.

16. Indyk, W. Psychology for screenwriters : building conflict into a story / W. Indyk. - Moscow: Alpina Non-Fiction, 2014. - 348 c.

17. Karchevskaya, K. S. Archetypes in cinematography : culturological analysis : autoref. dissertation for the degree of Candidate of Cultural Studies : 24.00.01 / K. S. Karchevskaya ; St. Petersburg State University. - St. Petersburg. , 2010. - 25 c.

18. Campbell, J. The hero with a thousand faces: myth. Archetype. Unconscious / J. Campbell. - K. : Sofia, 1997. - 335 c.

19. Lindgren, E. The art of cinema : an introduction to film studies / E. Lindgren. - M.: Izd. foreign lit., 1956. - 192 c.

20. Lunacharsky, A. V. Thirty-six dramatic plots / A. V. Lunacharsky // On theater and dramaturgy / A. V. Lunacharsky. - Moscow: Art, 1958. - VOL. II, PP. 113-117.

21. McKee, R. The million-dollar story / R. McKee. - M. : Alpina nonfiction, 2012. -

464 c.

22. Mitta, A. Cinema between hell and heaven: the cinema of Eisenstein, Chekhov, Shakespeare, Kurosawa, Fellini, Hitchcock, Tarkovsky.... / A. Mitta. - Moscow: Zebra E, 2005. - 480c.

23. Mythologeme of woman-judge at ancient Celts and Germans : collection of articles / edited by T.A.Mikhailova. - Moscow: Indrik, 2005. - 334 c.

24. The "irrelevant" genres. "Round Table" at the Russian Institute of Art History, St. Petersburg, April 2004 / Angelika Artyukh // Film Studies Notes - 2004. - № 69. - C. 150 - 174.

25. Proskurov, D. Blockbuster: archetypes and acts / D. Proskurov [Electronic resource]. - Mode of access : http://dmitryprosukov.blogspot.com/2009/02/blog-post.html Access date : 22.12.2014.

26. Reisen, O. K. Stray subjects in cinema / O. Reisen. - Moscow: Izd. firm "Materik", 2002. - 168 c.

27. Rossio, T. 20 mistakes an experienced screenwriter won't make / T. Rossio [Electronic resource]. - Mode of access : http://www.cinemotionlab.com/stati/20_oshibok,_kotorih_ne_sovershit_opitnii_scenarist/ Access date: 28.11.2014

28. Rutsky, E. A. Mythologie de la force impure dans la culture traditionnelle des Biélorusses / Eugene Rutsky // Authentic folklore : problems of vyvuchannya, zahavannya, peraimannya / J. Rutsk - Minsk : NBB - P. 78-80. 78-80.

29. Salynsky, D. Esquisses sur le problème des genres au cinéma / Dmitry Salynsky // Kinologicheskie zapiski - 2004. - № 69. - C. 175-203.

30. Salynsky, D. Composition memoir: the seven seconds and everything else /. Д. Salynsky [Electronic resource] - Access mode: http://www.kinozapiski.ru/ru/article/sendvalues/878/Дата access : 01.03.2015

31. Samutina, N. Intellectual auteur cinema as a European idea / N. Samutina [Electronic resource].- Mode of access:

http://www.kinozapiski.ru/ru/article/sendvalues/194/Дата access : 11.04.2015.
32. Screenwriting Mastery : Film and TV Dramaturgy as Art, Craft and Business : Ref.book by R.Walter / Institute for Advanced Training of Television and Radio Broadcasting Workers. - M. , 1993. - 63 c.
33. Tkachenko, I. Women who came from the cold. Scandinavian serials / I. Tkachenko [Electronic resource].- Mode of access: http://www.kinoart.ru/archive/2014/05/zhenshchiny-kotorye-prishli-s-кhoIodaДата access : 18.12.2014.
34. Turkina, V. G. Mythologeme of the hero and mass consciousness: Author's abstract of the thesis for the degree of Candidate of Philosophy : 09.00.11 / V. G. Turkina ; Saratov State University named after N.G. Chernyshevsky. N.G.Chernyshevsky. - Saratov, 2001. - 22 c.
35. Usmanova, O. S. A cinematic work of art as a space for intercultural dialogue : abstract of the dissertation for the candidate diploma in philosophical sciences : specialty 24.00.01 Theory and history of culture / O. S. Usmanova ; Kazan State University of Culture and Arts. - Kazan, 2012. - 20 c.
36. Freilich, S.I. Film theory : from Eisenstein to Tarkovsky : a handbook for universities / S.I. Freilich. - Moscow : Academic Project : Mir, 2007. - 508 c.
37. Fraser, J. J. Fraser, Folklore in the Old Testament / J. J. Fraser. - Moscow: Publishing House of Political Literature, 1989. - 542 c.
38. Hall, J. Dictionary of Plots and Symbols in Art / J. Hall. - M. : KRON-PRESS, 1996. - 656 c.
39. Khrenov, N. The cinema as a rehabilitation of archetypal reality / H. Khrenov [Electronic resource]. - Mode of access : http://www.kinozapiski.ru/ru/article/sendvalues/1000/Дата access : 21.02.2015.
40. Khrenov, N. Domestic cinematography: the rehabilitation of archetypes Reality / N. Khrenov [Electronic resource]. - Mode of access : http://www.kinozapiski.ru/ru/article/sendvalues/741/Дата access : 01.03.2015.
41. Erikson, E. The tragedy of personality / Erik Erikson. - M. : EXMO, 2008. - 256

c.

42. Sharapova, M. A. Archetypal bases of the hero image in the dramaturgy of Russian cinema (on film material from the years 1986-2012) : author's abstract of the thesis for the Candidate Degree in Art History : 17.00.03 / M. A. Sharapova ; All-Russian State University of Cinematography named after S. A. Gerasimov. S. A. Gerasimov. - Moscow, 2013. - 28 c.

43. Jung, K.G. Soul and myth Six archetypes / Carl Gustav Jung. - K. Ukrainian State Library for Young People, 1996. - 384 c.

44. Jung, K.G. On the archetypes of the collective unconscious / K.G. Jung - M. : Centre, 1997. - 243 c.

45. Yampolsky, M. B. The Visible World: Essays on Early Film Phenomenology / M. Boris. - Moscow: Research Institute of Cinematographic Art, 1993. - 216 c.

46. All-time box-office top 100 films [Electronic resource].- Access mode: http://www.filmsite.org/boxoffice.html - Access date: 20.04.2015.

47. All Time Highest Grossing Movies Worldwide [Electronic resource].- Mode of access: http://www.the-numbers.com/movie/records/All-Time-Worldwide-Box- Office - Date of access: 20.04.2015.

48. Characters as Device [Electronic resource]. - Mode of access : http://tvtropes.org/pmwiki/pmwiki.php/Main/CharactersAsDevice - Access date: 11.04.2015.

49. Corbett, D. Lifting the mask: types, archetypes and the casual human being/ David Corbett// Moviemaker. - 2014. - Issue 105, Vol. 20. - P. 22-24.

50. Gallagher, M. Action figures : men, action films, and contemporary adventure narratives / Mark Gallagher. - NY. : Palgrave Macmillan, 2007. - 234 p.

51. Grant, B.K. Film Genre : From Iconography to Ideology / Barry Keith Grant ; NY. : Wallflower Press, 2007. - 131 p.

52. Hill, G. Illuminating shadows : the mythic power of film / G. Hill. Hill. - Boston : Shambhala, 1992. - 319 p.

53. Hollis, J. Mythologems: Incarnations of the Invisible World / James Hollis. -

Toronto : Inner City Books, 2004. - 158 p.

54. Iaccino, J. F. Jungian Reflections Within the Cinema: A Psychological Analysis of Sci-fi and Fantasy Archetypes / J. F. Jungian Reflections Within the Cinema: A Psychological Analysis of Sci-fi and Fantasy Archetypes. F. Iaccino. - Santa Barbara: Greenwood Publishing Group, 1998. - 216 p.

55. Iaccino, J. F. Psychological Reflections on Cinematic Terror: Jungian Archetypes in Horror Films / J. F. Iaccino. F. Iaccino. - Westport : Praeger, 1994. - 232 p.

56. Langford, B. Film Genre: Hollywood and Beyond / Barry Langford. - Edinburgh: Edinburgh University Press, 2005. - 310 p.

57. Peary, G. The modern American novel and the cinema / G. Peary. Peary. - New York, 1978. - 461 p.

58. Shadid, B. The screenwriter's toolbox / Basil Shadid // Moviemaker. - 2014. - Issue 105, Vol. 20. - P. 16 - 20.

59. Sklar, R. Movie-made America : A cultural history of American movies / R. Sklar. Sklar. - NY. Vintage Books, 1994.

60. Sparling, C. Buried comes alive : one location is all it takes to create a comoelling story / Chris Sparling // Moviemaker. - 2011. - Issue 89, Volume 17. - P. 64 - 67.

61. Streett, B. The Astrology of Film : The Interface of Movies, Myth, and Archetype / B. Streett, J. Kishner. Streett, J. Kishner. - Bloomington : iUniverse, 2004. - 218 p.

62. Tasker, Y. The Hollywood action-adventure film / Y. Tasker. - Hoboken : John Wiley & Sons, 2015. - 224 p.

63. Truby J., Sell that script / John Truby// Moviemaker. - 2011. - Issue 89, Vol. 17 - P. 28 - 30.

64. Worldwide grosses [Electronic resource].- Mode d'accès : http://www.boxofficemojo.com/alltime/world/ - Date d'accès : 28.04.2015.

APPENDIX A
Terminology dictionary

Archetype (Greek, "first image", "original", "authentic work") - primary image, ancient form, prototype; a way of relating images passing from generation to generation, hidden in the collective unconscious common to all mankind; a set of innate, universal forms of the human imagination [Dictionary of Foreign Words of the Russian Language] ; in literary criticism, an original image, character or structure of circumstance recurring in literature, suggesting a fairly coherent universal concept of the development of the human imagination [Dictionary of Foreign Words of the Russian Language]. [Encyclopaedia Britannica].

Genre canon (Greek "canon" - "norm") - system of internal creative rules and norms, which set the basic structural and compositional regularities for the development of works in specific genres [Merriam-Webster/Britannica Thesaurus].

Genre convention - the accepted translation of "genre narrative" - is a terminological synonym for the concept of "genre canon" in foreign film studies and film production,

Myth (from Greek "legend", "tale", "story") - ancient folk tale about deified gods and heroes, about the origin of the universe and life on Earth [Dictionary of Foreign Words in the Russian Language]; legend about ancient pagan gods and heroes in the form of individual accounts of their lives [Complete Dictionary of Foreign Words in Use in the Russian Language]; symbolic narrative, as a rule, unknown.
associated with traditional folklore and religious tradition [Encyclopaedia Britannica].

Mythologeme (Greek "source/reason for legend/tale/story") - main or recurring theme of a myth, linear statement of the facts and events of a myth, mythological narrative [Merriam-Webster/Britannica Thesaurus]; constituent element of a mythological plot [Ushakov's Explanatory Dictionary]; similar, recurring theme in the myths of different peoples [Encyclopedic Dictionary].

Frame - the period (place in time), duration (length in time), location (place in space) and level of conflict (position in the hierarchy of social contradictions) **of** a story [R.McKee].

Main idea - the order and reasons for changes in situations that occur in the plot of a screenplay; the value and reason for an event [R.McKee].

APPENDIX B

Filmography

Ribbons for children and young people :

title	year	chrono footage	director	scenario
Spring fairy tale	1971	93 min	Yuri Tsvetkov	Yuri Tsvetkov
Kingfisher	1972	75 min	Vyacheslav Nikiforov	Yuri Yakovlev
Dirk	1973	210 min.	Nikolay Kalinin	Anatoly Rybakov
Bronze bird	1974	201 min.	Nikolay Kalinin	Anatoly Rybakov
The last summer of my childhood	1974	193 min	Valery Rubinchik	Anatoly Rybakov
The adventures of Pinocchio	1975	130 min	Leonid Nechayev	Inna Vetkina
About Little Red Riding Hood	1977	135 min.	Leonid Nechayev	Inna Vetkina
Laughter sold	1981	140 min.	Leonid Nechayev	Inna Vetkina
Summer impressions on Planet Z	1986	120 min.	Eugène Markovsky	Yuri Tomin
Flying to the country monsters	1986	73 min	Vladimir Bychkov	Vladimir Golovanov, Vladimir Golovanov
Peter Pan	1987	135 min.	Leonid Nechayev	Elena Barinova
New Year's adventures in July	2008	72 min	Ivan Pavlov, Elena Turova	Elena Turova
Carrot Top in the mirror	2010	120 min.	Elena Turova	Elena Turova
Incredible displacement	2014	90 minutes	Alexander Anisimov	Margarita Shagrai

Heroic and patriotic ribbons:

title	year	timing	director	scenario
The ruins fire at close range	1970	390 min.	Vitaly Chetverikov	Ivan Novikov, Ivan Chigrinov
State border. We are ours, we are new...	1980	133 min.	Boris Stepanov	Alexei Nagorny, Heli Ryabov
State border. A peaceful Summer 21	1980	133 min.	Boris Stepanov	Alexei Nagorny, Heli Ryabov
State border. Eastern border	1982	145 min.	Boris Stepanov	Alexei Nagorny, Heli Ryabov
State border. Red sand	1984	140 min.	Boris Stepanov	Alexei Nagorny, Heli Ryabov
State border. Year 41	1986	134 min.	Vyacheslav Nikiforov	Oleg Smirnov
State border. Beyond the threshold of victory	1987	136 min.	Boris Stepanov	Oleg Smirnov
State border. Salt wind	1988	128 min	Gennady Ivanov	Oleg Smirnov
State border. On the remote border	1988	128 min	Gennady Ivanov	Piotr Lucik, Alexei Samoryadov, Oleg Smirnov
title	**year**	**timing**	**director**	**scenario**
You have a mission	2004	78 min	Yuri Berzhitsky	Alena Kalyunova, Mykola Cherginets
Shield of the homeland	2007	80 min	Denis Skvortsov	Alexander Myshalov
June 1941.	2008	200 min	Alexandre Franskiewicz-Laye	Sergei Ashkenazi, Stanislav Govorukhin,

Adventurous Tapes :

title	year	timing	director	scenario
Time waits for no man	1975	152 min.	Vitaly Chetverikov	И. Kornev
Half-Life	2011	16 min	Daria Zhuk	Justin Lieberman, Michael Pitch
Confusing the issue	2014	110 min	Ivan Maslyukov	Ivan Maslyukov

Detective tapes :

title	year	timing	director	scenario
King Stach's wild hunt	1979	139 min.	Valery Rubinchik	Vladimir Korotkevich, Valery Rubinchik
Black lock Olshansky	1984	127 min.	Mikhail Ptashuk	Vladimir Korotkevich
August forty. fourth	2001	118 min.	Mikhail Ptashuk	Vladimir Bogomolov
In the footsteps of the apostles	2013	208 min.	Sergey Talybov	Oleg Sukhamera, Viktor Lobkovich

Activists :

title	year	timing	director	scenario
The Nuclear Ranger	1999	85 min	Vyacheslav Nikiforov	Valentin Chernykh
Sniper: Firearms retaliation	2001	163 minutes.	Alexander Efremov	Gleb Shprygov
A deadly battle	2010	167 min.	Alexandre Franskiewicz-Laye	Andrei Kureychik

Horror films :

title	year	timing	director	scenario
Masakra	2010	100 min	Andrei Kudinenko	Alexander Kachan

MIX
Papier aus verantwortungsvollen Quellen
Paper from responsible sources
FSC® C105338

Printed by Books on Demand GmbH, Norderstedt / Germany